M000032712

chester gigolo

diary of a dog star

Christina Potter

Aperture Press

Copyright © 2012 by Christina Potter

All rights reserved. Published by Aperture Press. Name and associated logos are trademarks and/or registered trademarks of Aperture Press, LLC.

No part of this publication may be reproduced, stored in a retrieval system, or transmitted in any form or by any means, electronic, mechanical, photocopying, recording, or otherwise, without written permission of the publisher. For information, write to Aperture Press, P.O. Box 6485, Reading, PA 19610 or visit www.AperturePress.net.

ISBN 978-0-9850026-8-8

Library of Congress Control Number: 2012943462

Printed in the U.S.A.

First Edition, July 2012

Cover and interior design by Stephen Wagner.
Cover and interior photos by Taylor "Sherm" Potter, courtesy of ShermanArts Photography.

*This book is dedicated to our beautiful Afghan
Hound Desi who left us unexpectedly,
shortly after Chester joined our family.*

*Thank you, Desi, for all you taught me and for
introducing me to so many wonderful dog people.*

chester gigolo

Introduction

My name is Crestview Grand Duke of Chester Gigolo,
but Mom and Dad call me Chester. I am a Berger Picard,
a noble French herding dog. For those of you unfamiliar
with Picards, don't panic, you are not alone. We are an
uncommon ancient breed, brought to northern France in
the ninth century. My ancestors almost became extinct
during World War II and there are still fewer than 4,500
of us worldwide. Most of my relatives reside in France.
We are loyal, loving and have an exceptional sense of humor, though some would say that our stubborn streak can
be trying at times.

I was born in New Jersey to hard working parents.
Parents who obviously should have used birth control as,
shortly after we were born, it was decided that we would
all be given up for adoption. Luckily, I found a home with
a lovely couple; their names are Mom and Dad. I have
three siblings: a Golden Retriever named Kelly, her biological grandson named Hudson, and a hairless Chinese
Crested named Morgan. Morgan has hair on her tail,
neck and feet, yet they call her kind *hairless*—don't ask.

Kelly doesn't seem to enjoy my company, maybe because I'm a bit rambunctious for her. She is probably as patient with me as you can expect a fifteen-year-old Golden to be. Hudson and I are very close, he is my best friend... or as Mom would say, my *co-defendant*.

Mom is an interpreter and translator who works mostly in courts. I know from the stories I hear that you do not want to end up on the wrong side of the law. You must stay on the right side of the law. I always stay to the right of everything just to be safe. Dad is an airline pilot. He's gone more often than I'd like so I may ask him to switch to a nine-to-five job. We have a home that would otherwise be lovely, were it not for the lack of yard. I've put up a "for sale" sign in hopes of moving out of our apartment into something more appropriate for our lifestyle. So far I've not gotten any offers.

We have very busy lives. I, myself, am an athlete, actor and author. Though I've dabbled in other professions, I believe I've found my niche. I thoroughly enjoy sports. I've successfully competed in Rally obedience and am preparing for agility. Agility is a team sport in which a dog guides his human companion through an obstacle course. If they run it without errors, it's called a clean run. That sounds easier than it is because not only do we have to communicate with our "handlers", we also have to negotiate the obstacles while doing so. The handlers just run alongside us and sometimes get in our way.

I hope to take a shot at conformation also, that's the canine equivalent of a beauty pageant. Get this, if you win in the conformation ring and you're a boy, they call you Winners Dog (WD), but if you're a girl they call you Winners Bitch (WB). Morgan is a conformation champion which means that she's been called a bitch many times.

On the pages that follow, you can read about some of the experiences and adventures that I encountered during the first year of my life.

I'm dedicating this book to my beautiful Afghan Hound sister Desi who, sadly, is no longer with us.

Notes From A B.P. Puppy

Hi everyone, my name is Chester. I am a twelve-week-old Berger Picard puppy who weighs 23.4 pounds and measures seventeen inches at the withers. Now that I seem to have settled into my new digs, I must get down to serious writing business to keep you all abreast of what's been going on since I arrived at my new home.

Even though I couldn't be cuter or more cuddly, my sisters all seem to dislike me—not sure why. Kelly snaps at me, Morgan growls at me, and Desi... well, suffice it to say I make sure to stay away from her. Thank goodness for H, a.k.a. Hudson. He is one cool dude. I am learning a lot from him and can tell that he still has a lot more to teach. He has infinite patience with me. He's very down to earth for someone with his success. Mental note: don't let fame go to your head. People will admire you all the better.

Anyway, since I got here, there has been a lot of training and playing. I already know how to sit, down, come, kennel up, wait, put my front paws on things, kiss, turn left, turn right, say my prayers, lift my paw, and take a bow, all on command. Oh, I also retrieve... you don't live with two Golden Retrievers without learning a thing or two!

My biggest success so far was at ten and a half weeks—I had my first media job *and* learned to speak on command. Mom and Dad are very impressed; they keep telling everyone that they've never had a puppy learn to speak on command at such a young age, in just two days and with only twenty minutes' worth of training. Hmm, I must be all that and a bag of chips! By the way, the media job was for "Company Kids" Christmas catalog... maybe I'll make the cover... won't I be the envy of the dog park!

Ears Up!

July 10

I met a lovely chap by the name of Zorro yesterday. Well, I'd met him before but wasn't allowed to socialize with him... Mom said something about my shots. I'm not sure what she was talking about; I tuned her out because it was boring. Anyway, this Zorro character is much older than I am—he's six weeks older, so he's also more worldly than I. Mom explained that he looks different because he's a Collie. I found him intriguing, possibly due to the permanent mask he was wearing. Lovely young man, I sure hope he'll be up to some friendly competition in the agility ring next year.

Hudson told me about two interesting gentlemen he admired when he was young; a Standard Poodle by the name of Mr. Satchi and an Afghan Hound named Mr. Trey. I believe I've seen Mr. Satchi at agility trials, though we didn't get a chance to shoot the breeze at the time. We're not sure what ever became of Mr. Trey, he was a hippy so he probably got into trouble and ended up in detention somewhere in Connecticut.

In any event, it was nice to spend the weekend at an

agility trial and get away from the chaos we had at home this week. We had new wood floors installed so there were plenty of interesting sounds, people and equipment to investigate, and I quite enjoyed it. I am, it would seem, most inquisitive. Speaking of... I was introduced to my first body of water yesterday: a stream. I didn't hesitate to see what it was all about. I went right in. Again, Mom and Dad were impressed by my reaction. They seem to impress easily, these two. I, too, was impressed upon awakening and seeing my reflection Friday morning. You see, my ears were both upright. I quite like this new me—fascinating.

Life's A Beach!

July 17

What an *awesome* day I had yesterday! Mom and Dad took me to the beach with Hudson and Morgan. Hudson and I went swimming and I loved it. I am without a doubt the best non-fowl swimmer this side of the Mississippi. What do you expect from a dog with paws the size of flippers? And my tootsies are webbed. Yes! Webbed! "Why?" you ask. I don't really know. I'm not a water dog, yet my tremendous paws are webbed like it's nobody's business. Why would a canine that's suppose to tend to ungulates have webbed pedes? I'll have to do a Google search and get back to you.

Anyhow, I wasn't sure if I should jump in at first. After all, the only other times I've seen water was in the bathtub (yuck!) and a somewhat muddy stream last weekend. This body of water was ginormous and there was some green grassy stuff floating in it; I believe they told me it was seaweed. It was wicked slimy and I quite liked the look and feel of it. So, Dad throws this ball in and there goes Hudson, splashing away. Well, not to be outdone, I bravely jump in behind him. Water is everywhere; I become momentarily submerged... Then, like the mighty Loch Ness monster, out I jump! All twenty-nine sopping wet pounds of me! I shake the water off and am flung off my feet by the violent flopping of my gargantuan ears. I know I must be a frightful sight, yet, who cares? This is so invigorating. "Throw the ball again! Throw the ball again!" I shout. Dad obliges and off we go, Hudson impetuously launches into the ocean with me close behind him. At times I get the ball; at times I let him get it. The excitement is intoxicating—Hudson and I don't want the fun to end. Alas, at their age Mom and Dad tire easily and call an all-too-premature end to the festivities. I shall cherish these memories forever!

Daydreaming

04

This week was overflowing with psychological drama for me due to the fact that I got myself most unnecessarily flustered, all thirty-one pounds of me. You see, one day, out of nowhere, Mom says "We're going to start training you for your RN." My head starts spinning and I am momentarily unable to comprehend or even hear any other words coming out of her mouth. RN? A nurse? Is she serious? Has she completely lost her mind? For heaven's sake, I'm a dog; stop anthropomorphizing me! Listen, I'm as intelligent, compassionate and caring as the next guy but, really, a nurse? Doesn't that reek of tee many martoonis to you?

After the initial shock, however, I decide to give it some thought. Despite the fact that I lack the opposable thumbs needed to perform certain Florence Nightingalean tasks— such as giving shots, opening bottles of pills, taking blood pressure, or even holding a pen—perhaps I can make up for these shortcomings with my tremendous God-given talents. After all, I am a shepherd and our instinct is to care for those in need. Also, I am extraordinarily gifted at non-verbal communication so that wouldn't be an issue. Hmm, a nurse? Can I actually do this? I'll have to research it, but I'm almost positive that I would be the first dog to become a nurse. I'd most definitely go down in history. I can see the headlines now: "Jersey Picard graduates from Princeton with Honors." Not just national headlines, no no, *international* headlines as well—on every continent. I'd be the talk of the town; indeed, the talk of *every* town. How do you say "nurse" in Ket? Esperanto? Tasmanian? Dogri? From there, the possibilities would be endless. Think of all the good I could do. Fame and fortune would knock on my door, no doubt. Everyone would be extremely impressed.

On the other thumbless hand (pun intended), do I really want to spend an inordinate amount of time studying? What would Hudson do while I hit the books? I'm sure he'd miss our play sessions; I know I would. Nursing may not be the career for me after all. I suppose that I now need to find a way to break this most disagreeable news to...

"Chester, Chester!" Mom says impatiently. "Come on, let's go practice your sits, downs, waits." Hang on a second, did she mean rally? Is that the RN to which she was referring? A Rally Novice title? Oh, I guess that explains the extra training sessions built around attention games. Perhaps, that, too, is the reason Dad had me going over something he kept calling a "jump". Hey, don't panic, even if I don't make my mark at Princeton, I will make it in canine competitive events... CH OTCH MACH Chester RAE, hey, a guy's gotta dream.

There were two events worthy of mention this week:

Firstly, I visited one of my birth brothers. His name is Solo; he's dark, brindle like my biological father. (Did I mention that I'm adopted?) I take after my biological mom in that I'm fawn colored.

There are other differences between us besides the physical ones. He told me that he goes to school; I'm home schooled. He's got a lovely yard; I'm walked on a leash. He doesn't have to work; I'm an actor. He exercises for fun; I'm a professional athlete. However, he's got no brothers with whom to tussle, with whom to play fetch, from whom to learn the ropes. Me, I've got Hudson! Enough said, I've got the better life.

Secondly, I saw myself in the mirror again. Now that I'm taller, I am able to look at myself in the bathroom mirrors at will. So when I caught my reflection this week, I had to ask myself, "Self, is this stunning reflection of an ideal representation of a Berger Picard really me?" I was transfixed. Wow! Those upright ears—four and a half inches of perfection. Those expressive eyes—full of love.

The inquisitive tilt of my perfectly sized head--flawless. I could barely look away. I also noticed that I seem to be growing a mustache and beard. I shan't shave them off, this look is dashing, masculine! It suits me. I think Hudson is a bit envious.

I, on the other paw, envy his teeth. I've lost some, you see. I noticed it when I looked in the mirror. Three or four of them—gone. Mysteriously! I can't find them anywhere. Perhaps it would behoove me to find out if I really lost them... or if they were actually stolen!

Was I the victim of a toothless thief? Or, were they pilfered by someone looking to make a quick buck by fencing them on the street? What would be the punishment for this type of crime? Incarceration, no doubt. I must find out if they were lost or stolen before filing a police report. The only flaw in my plan to investigate this heinous crime, if, in fact, one was committed, is that I don't know where to start. It might be difficult to lift fingerprints from my muzzle and/or remaining teeth. Do I call the local CSI office? What would you do? I'm open to suggestions...

The Great Tooth Caper

August 07

Wow, how quickly the weeks pass. I am now almost four months old, can you believe it? Me neither. And get this, almost twenty inches at the withers and about thirty-eight pounds! Now, I don't want to beat a dead horse, nor a live one, for that matter. Actually, there's no need to beat any animal if you think about it, nor eat them, nor abuse them in any way. As a matter of fact, Mom's friend Judy works for American Humane to ensure that animals are properly treated. She sounds like a lovely woman; I can't wait to meet her. I haven't met her yet because she lives in another country; I think it's called Los Angeles.

Anyway, I digress. I don't want to beat the proverbial dead horse, but the tooth situation deserves another diary entry this week. I've been extra vigilant with regards to my teeth (my image, after all!), yet more have gone missing! I was unsure as to whether they'd been misplaced or pilfered until I noticed that Morgan was missing some as well. Coincidence? I think not! I no longer suspect foul play, no, no, I don't suspect it. I *know* it's foul play!

I decided the matter warranted further investigation

so I put in a call to the local Sheriff's Department requesting assistance, to no avail. Then I tried CSI, NYPD, CIA,
FBI, NYU, HSN, UAL, MSRP—every acronym of which
I could think—even though I don't know what most of
those mean. They all sounded important so what the
heck, a call couldn't hurt, right?

Not one of them returned my calls. Are they purpose-
fully turning a blind eye? Could this be something larger
than one toothless thief? Even larger than an entire gang
of toothless tooth dealers? I'll tell you one thing, it's definitely interstate. I received an e-mail from my colleague
and Collie (ha, ha) Zorro. You know, the one who resides
in Connecticut. He tells me that someone has also absconded with some of his teeth. Perhaps it's some sort of
conspiracy... International tooth trafficking, perhaps?

I'd never heard of it and I know it sounds ludicrous.
I myself wouldn't have believed it if I wasn't involved;
but it's true I tell you! Maybe I can get to the bottom
of this and write a piece for the local newspaper, or a
book! OMG, I smell a movie-of-the-week, "The Canine's
Canines Caper"! Get it? It could star yours truly and
some young, gorgeous, leggy lassie whom I would personally cast. Oh, and Hudson would co-star. I might even
be persuaded to give the girls (Kelly, Desi and Morgan)
small, non-speaking parts. Okay, before my imagination
starts, I mean, continues wandering, let me tell you about
the other step I've taken to solve this nefarious crime: I've

made a list of names of would-be conspirators. Everyone is a suspect. Trust no one. Yes, *your* name is on it! I've seen enough cop shows to know that I must not let my emotions get in the way. So far I've only been able to remove two names. Mine, and thanks to cousin Debbie's advice, Morgan's was the other. If Morgan (my little Crested sister) had stolen my teeth, she wouldn't have sold them as she needs them just as much as I do. No, she most certainly would have gone to a first rate dentist to have them implanted in her own mouth. Well, I checked when she was sleeping today and she is still missing teeth. And if I would've taken them, we wouldn't be having this conversation, would we? Would we? *Would we?!?* Hello, pay attention!

So, Morgan's and my names have been removed from said list. Anywho, in the spirit of friendship, I am giving *you*—you know who you are—a chance to return said teeth, no questions asked. You have one week. Una semana. You may return them in the same sneaky, snake-like, stealthy fashion you used to lift them. If said teeth don't find their way to their rightful owner within seven days, I shall be forced to revisit this subject in my next entry!

Case Closed!

August 14

Good news! For my four-month birthday, my teeth were returned! Yes! *And* they're bigger than ever and seem to be growing daily. Were they injected with growth hormones or harvested in some fashion? Just when I thought I'd have to take desperate measures, such as implants, here they are, back where they belong. Oh, before I forget, thanks for the suggestion, Sandy, but it looks like dentures will not be necessary after all. It might behoove you to keep that suggestion handy for your soon-to-be-adopted Crested girl. In any event, the tooth matter can finally be put to rest. No need to revisit it.

In the interim, however, Hudson told me something about a certain lady named "the Tooth Fairy"; I wonder if she had anything to do with the return? Or, is she, in a desperate attempt to make a name for herself, the one who absconded with them in the first place? You know the drill, she takes them and then gets credit for returning them. I've heard about this before. People will do some crazy things in the interest of fame. Me, I don't need to resort to cheap tricks and/or engage in slightly illegal endeavors, I was born to be successful. Just wait and see. Perhaps not as a nurse and perhaps not at Princeton, but I will make a name for myself—mark my words! Regardless of the manner in which the teeth were returned, I must keep my promise of "no questions asked". There will be no further investigation, case closed.

Anyway, I am ecstatic that I can now return to my furniture chewing duties. It was difficult for a while there to really sink my teeth into stuff without, well, teeth. Perhaps that's the reason I was a bit on edge. I have now successfully left my mark on almost every piece of furniture in the house. I am so proud of myself. Unfortunately, judging from their reactions, I don't think that Mom and Dad are as proud of me as I am. I wonder why.

Speaking of... my biological mom, DD, and biological sister, Fanny, came to visit me last Sunday and I could tell from the looks in their eyes that *They* were proud of me. I was at an agility trial showing my support for my little Crested sister, Morgan, and my Golden brother, Hudson. They're fierce competitors; both on their way to their MACHs and need my support more than ever. What's a MACH you ask? How should I know? I'm only four months old; didn't you read that at the beginning of my diary? What do you want from me? It's all I can do to learn the thirty million other things my parents expect me to learn and now you want me to know what a MACH is? Good grief, hang on... let me Google it... just a minute... the computer's a bit slow. Hmm... this doesn't make sense... speed of sound... master agility—oh, I see, it's an agility championship. Cool, I think I shall get me one of those too.

Now, where was I? Oh yes, DD and Fanny came to visit. Wait! Before I continue, it's imperative that I clarify one thing. I wasn't going to mention it because I'm a bit embarrassed; however, in the interest of full disclosure, I must admit that Fanny is not really my sister. She's my half sister. It seems my biological dad, Aero, is a bit of a womanizer. I'm not surprised, he is one striking devil; tall, dark and handsome, with a personality to match his outstanding looks. I suppose that if one is to have a reputation, being a womanizer is not that ba—*ouch!* Mom! Okay, okay, sorry. Being a womanizer IS bad. Good grief, why are you reading over my shoulder anywa—*ouch!*

Now where was I? Oh, DD and Fanny visited and what an impression they made. How many times did Mom have to answer, "they're Picards, a French herding breed; yes, a rare breed...very good temperament. About 23–25 inches and 50–70 pounds"... The questions just kept pouring in. The "what are they?" question intrigued me because Mom *and* Dad were *both* wearing t-shirts that said "I love my Berger Picard". Hmmm.

Some people seem to ask the most axiomatic questions. I read once that the average man uses 2,000–4,000 words a day and the average woman uses 6,000–8,000.

Mom says it's because men don't listen the first time so women have to repeat everything. At least I think that's what she said; I wasn't really listening. Here's my point: if the average person didn't ask questions for which the answers are apparent—such as when you call the fire department and they ask "is there a fire?", or when the moving truck's in front of your house and the neighbor asks "are you moving?", and who hasn't been stopped, suitcase in hand with the inane "are you going on a trip?" question. You see my point, don't you? You don't? Well, here it is in a nutshell. If the average person didn't waste words with 'in-my-spare-time-I-split-the-atom' type questions, wouldn't it stand to reason that they would have those unused words readily available for more consequential topics?

The Naked Chef-ster

Now that I have the proper teeth required to chew almost anything to bits and, as I have already left stellar tooth marks on every piece of wood (furniture, baseboard, cabinets) in the house, Mom is teaching me how to cook. Once I learn the very limited amount she can teach me about cooking, I will apply to New York Culinary School. I've heard some great things about it and know for a fact that many talented chefs graduate from there all the time. I would love to attend, though I'm not sure if they will accept me. Don't get me wrong, I'm exactly the type of guy that these institutions strive to recruit; the talented, creative individual whose mere presence will serve to enrich their student body. The problem is that they may need to find a way to get around those pesky health codes. It seems that dealing with health officials can be quite a headache, a lot of bureaucratic nonsense, a great deal of paperwork, and oodles of wasted time. Do I really want to go through all that? And if they do accept me, how will I finance it? Can I get a loan? Banks are not exactly jonesing to give money to high risk individuals. At my age and without a work history, they may see me as a high risk individual. Again, I'll have to fill out tons of paperwork, answer countless questions, even put something up for collateral.

The collateral part isn't a problem. I have a few collaterals; the one I'm wearing now is black and matches my leash. Nah, you know what? That all sounds like too much work and I don't have the patience for it so maybe culinary school isn't such a great idea after all. In any event, I'm not sure that Mom is teaching me how to cook as voluntarily as I'd like. She seems to be a bit put out when I try to help. I grab a utensil, she pulls it away. I take a piece of food from the kitchen counter, she gives me "the look". I sniff at plates on the counter and lick the food, again with "the look". She's perfected "the look" and I have perfected "the ignore". It's quite the symbiotic relationship.

The kitchen towel is another matter, we have so much fun with it. You should see how Mom chases me through the house when I take it. Her cries of "Chester, leave it!" always put a smile on my face! Wait a minute, maybe that means that she doesn't want me to take it? Could it possibly be off limits too? Well, that would explain the frustrated pleas I hear behind me as I run away, butt tucked under, slipping on the wood floors, slamming into furniture, knocking precious knick-knacks to and fro. I laugh every time I imagine her chasing me; we get such good exercise. Am I the only one enjoying these "play sessions"? Mom doesn't seem to have much play drive. I constantly hear things like "Stay away from the hot pan", "Don't bite the furniture", "Stop chasing Morgan", "Don't run out open doors"... geez, these people have a lot of rules! I think I'll ask some of my dog friends if this is the norm or if our house is an exception. The first one I'll ask is my Malamute friend Dasher. He is self assured and honest. He's a quiet dude, yet not one to mince words. You know the type, no idle chit chat. I know I can trust him to provide me with candid advice. I'll have to ideate what measures to take should Dasher tell me that my household is too strict. Should I run away? If so, I'd need to pack my toys and collaterals, but how do you pull a suitcase zipper without opposable thumbs? I'm not grabbing it with my teeth, you know how I cherish them. Maybe I should just stick around and convince Hudson and the girls to picket with me. I might even call the teamsters. I'd better not make any rash decisions. I shall wait until I have all the facts to determine my next course of action.

Dinner And A Movie 09

This week I discovered feature films. I had no idea theaters existed. I mean, I've watched television many times and home videos, too. My favorite home video subject being, surprisingly, me! I really enjoy watching myself because I look exquisite on TV—imagine how much more formidable I would look on the silver screen. I'd probably have to get a stage name such as Chesterton Potter or Duke Chesterfield so as not to be hounded, *ha, ha*, by paparazzi in my personal time. I've heard they can be quite specious.

My pseudonym, as it were, would have to be something with an intriguing, yet easy-to-remember, ring to it. Though nothing too common like Lassie or Benji. I'm not sure what name Hudson uses for his acting gigs; it's never come up. Maybe he can advise me. I'll have to ask him.

Anyway, the feature film I saw was "Our Idiot Brother". Mom and Dad were so excited to see it that I had to find out what all the fuss was about. Going to the movies wasn't as easy as I thought it would be. I sat by the front door at home, as is my modus operandi when I want to go out, but Mom and Dad walked out right past me and shut the door! Well, I was having none of that, so I started barking up a storm and they assumed that I needed to go out to "do my business", which is really none of anyone's business. When they brought me back inside, I strategically placed a toy between the door frame and the door. I purposely chose a quiet toy as I knew that my squawking chicken toys would draw attention to my diabolical plan. Out went Mom and Dad, and, though they thought that the door was closed, voila! I pushed it open and was able to sneak out behind them.

The theater they go to is walking distance from home so I followed them. I had to use as much natural cover as I could: trees, tall grass, parked cars, you know, blend in just in case they should turn around and catch me in flagrante delicto. Though that in itself was tricky, what I didn't realize was that getting into the theater would present a bigger challenge. Inquiring eyes everywhere! Even with my flawless disguise of t-shirt, shorts and sunglasses, (no need for fake mustache and beard, I have genuine ones) I managed to surreptitiously walk past the ticket booths. I must admit I had a bit of trouble figuring out which of the eighteen theaters was showing the movie in question. I can't read as proficiently as you might think, yet. However, I found the correct theater and thankfully the lights were already out, so I walked in. I'm now twenty-one inches at the withers and needed to go unnoticed, a somewhat arduous task. I decided I should lay down in the front row so as to make myself all but imperceptible, and then all of a sudden... previews! The excitement was palpable; all that action, oh my! I was entranced. At times I wanted to stand up and clap. At one point I got so excited that I actually *did* stand up. Suddenly some nimrod in the back yelled , "Hey you, the one with the hat that looks like ginormous ears, either take it off or sit down!" How rude was that? He was patently jealous. I mean, come on, can you imagine my ears on the big screen? Twenty feet of impeccably bred, well set perfection.

After the previews came the feature film. I was mesmerized by the tremendousness of it all. To have so many well known actors starring in it, including... drum roll please... our very own Hudson! Yes, Hudson co-stars! Hudson's biological father Gable (may he rest in peace) has a co-starring and somewhat larger roll than Hudson does. Hudson's grandmother, Kelly, who is Gable's mother, also co-stars. The story is about Ned, played by Paul Rudd. He reminded me of myself: trusting, loyal, easygoing and friendly. Ned is an innocent and well-meaning chap who seemingly has turrets. I apparently suffer from that at times as well. If something needs to be said, why filter it? Just let it flow right up the throat, over the tongue, look out gums, here it comes! No need to go through the brain first, that's just a waste of time.

Ned has a dog named Willie Nelson (my Golden

siblings all playing the same character) and, through admittedly some fault of his own, he loses custody of Willie Nelson. The poor guy then spends the next hour and a half trying to reunite with his best friend. Quite touching and poignant. Gable didn't have any speaking parts which made his acting all the more formidable. I so enjoyed this, my first visit to the theater, that I shall go back; perhaps turn this into a weekly outing, maybe start a tradition. By the way, did you know that they have food there? Oh my gosh, yes, they have hot dogs, pizza, pretzels, all the junk food my little heart could ever dream of. I can feel my tummy rumbling just by thinking about it. Next time I'll do dinner and a movie, unless... yikes, those dreaded health codes hinder my night out, in which case, I'll have to sneak in a soda or maybe just do Netflix.

E. Coli Anyone?

September 04

Hi everybody,

I now weigh a lean forty-five pounds. I've developed some lovely muscles, in no small part thanks to my play sessions with Hudson—literally non stop. Dad seems somewhat put out by our play schedule at times. Is it the running through the house, the barking when he's trying to watch TV, the jumping on furniture, or the constantly wanting him to join us that annoys him? Does it really matter? All I know is that besides playing with Hudson, I've been having loads of fun playing with my new toys. There are so many that I cannot possibly write about all of them without getting bored or without boring you, so here is a sampling—these are the four that are especially chew worthy. They make these crazy sounds when thrown or squished, something like "aaaaaaaaaaaaahh-hhhhgggg", you'd have to hear it in person to really appreciate it. It's almost as if you burned your hand and it caught you by surprise; you know what I mean? It's hysterical! Anyway, the four toys of which I speak are chickens and they have names. No, I didn't name them and neither did Mom. Sure, Mom's two screws short of a tool shed but she didn't name these toys. They actually arrived with name tags and explanations of their personalities.

First is Earl. He's from Memphis and is a true chick magnet. As you can imagine, being from Memphis he is an Elvis impersonator, though not a very good one. I mean, really, an Elvis impersonator that wears shorts and a wife beater? He's got no class this one. He actually has a tattoo that says "mom" on his less-than-taught bicep. Cover it up, Earl! Plus, I heard Dad commenting on Earl's lack of "blew sway chews"; don't know what that means, but anything chewable is aces in my book.

Second is Chictoria. This girl is all elegance. Her designer black dress not only serves to accentuate her full bussom—definitely implants—but also highlights her poshness. I think she's British because she has a very tasteful tattoo of a British flag on her back. I know what you're thinking, however you're wrong. It's not a tramp stamp. It's up higher, right between the chicken wings, ha, ha. From what I hear, Chictoria is married to a soccer player; I believe his name is Beakham.

Third is Henrietta, tres sexy. She is a playchick bunny retired from Vegas and none too soon, as she's a bit past her prime. You could say she's overcooked, if you catch my drift. She still wears the bunny outfit; apparently the poor thing cannot let go of her past. Her "playchick" ears are ginormous, yet exceedingly attractive... hmm... who do they remind me of?

Fourth, and perhaps my personal favorite, is Jeff E. Coli. He is so cool that he has a middle name, just like I do. He's a blond surfer dude, though I haven't been able to figure out how he would paddle out to sea with those chicken wings of his. I'm a fantastic swimmer; remember we covered that topic in my diary, week three? As I told you then, I have the athletic build for it. Jeff, however, isn't built for swimming. As a matter of fact, he's not built for any sport that requires upper arm strength of any kind. How would you swim with those itty bitty extremities? Even if he laid flush with the edge of the surf board he would not be able to dip those short wings into the water, let alone paddle. Hmm, the more I think about it, the more this is starting to bother me.

I'm perplexed. How does Jeff do it? Does he have an agreement with local dolphins to pull him out to sea in order to catch a wave and hang six? We obviously have another mystery, a la tooth caper, on our paws. Oh my, is Jeff lying about his true identity? Maybe he's undercover with the FBI. An informant perhaps? Is he in the Federal Witness Protection Program? That would explain his chronic use of sunglasses, wouldn't it?

Okay, gotta go. I'm going to fill the tub, put Jeff on a spatula and see how he handles himself. What do you think? Will he sink, swim, or float around at the mercy of yours truly?

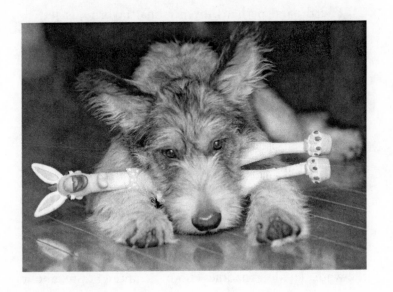

A Muppet's Life For Me

11

As I wrote a couple of weeks ago, I saw "Our Idiot Brother". What I failed to mention, because I was somewhat perturbed at the time, is that they re-shot the ending with an impostor.

The original ending was perfect. In it, Ned, Billy and our Gable drive off in a pick-up truck while bantering back and forth about nothing in particular. In the new ending, not only did they cut that witty Gable scene, but they also used a Golden that doesn't even look like him, leaving the audience to ponder the meaning of life!

Anyway, ever since seeing "Our Idiot Brother", I've been thinking about my silver screen debut and doing in-depth research—thus my impressive turn as a film critic. The other day, while lost in thought, much like Air Supply was Lost in Love, and after I'd had a particularly rough night, Mom told me I looked like a Muppet. You think that would've offended me but I wasn't really paying attention and didn't know what she meant anyway. After a couple of hours, I thought about what she'd said and decided to Google "Muppets" just in case I should have to give her the stink eye for the rest of the day. It wouldn't be the first time, though I'm not sure Mom was aware of it the other times, which made my efforts go all but unnoticed.

Fortunately, I liked what I discovered about the Muppets so no smelly sight organ was warranted. After oodles more research, I decided that in order to launch my movie career, I'd audition for the next Muppet movie. I've been watching the Muppets a lot lately and believe that their message of friendship is just the right vehicle for me; after all, I am all about friends and socializing. I'm a character actor so I will audition for one of the existing characters as opposed to requesting they create a new one just for me. I'm open to playing any of the Muppets with one caveat, I refuse to play Kermit. I don't understand what all the fuss is about and definitely don't care for the idea of spending countless hours in the makeup chair turning green (how do you wash that off anyway?) or taping my ears down—hello, they're two of my best features! Plus, he's just a frog for crying out loud. Come on, he grew up in a pond, probably a scummy one for all we know. And what's the deal with him and that swine? How's that relationship suppose to work? I don't get it and I definitely don't want to be a part of it.

In light of that, I've narrowed it down to three characters: Animal, Fozzie Bear and Sprocket. Animal and I have a lot in common: he's a primitive drummer and

I'm a primitive breed. He plays with "Dr. Teetha and The Electric Mayhem" and most likely gets all the babes. They seem to go for musicians. I play with "Baron von Hudson de Ville" and get all the babes too, even though I'm not a musician. However, I'm a bit concerned about Animal's apparent lack of oral hygiene, he's missing a bunch of teeth. Has he never heard of dentures? You know that now that I've found all my teeth, I want to show them off. I certainly don't look forward to having them blacked out for a movie role, no matter how big. That means that he's out of the question.

Next is Fozzie Bear. Fozzie is an endearing gent with a white bow tie similar to my natural black neck markings. He's well dressed. Hmm... I wonder if he's sponsored by a well known clothing brand? I could use some new designer duds... and shoes; I love shoes! I chew Mom and Dad's every chance I get. I'm an equal opportunity shoe chewer; Payless or Louboutin, it makes no difference to me. Made in China or Italy, chewable is chewable. But I digress. My biggest beef with Fozzie is that he's best friends with Kermit. Like I said before, I refuse to condone anything amphibian. I guess that narrows it down to Sprocket, who was actually my favorite to begin with. You see, Sprocket and I have a lot in common: he is a herding dog and so am I; he is intelligent and my recently tested IQ is 147; he has beautiful bushy eyebrows and so does yours truly; he's got the 'stache and beard and... well, suffice it to say,

I'm the envy of the dog park. So, Sprocket it is. With minimal makeup and a few sessions with an acting coach (you know, to hone my natural acting abilities), I will make Sprocket the Al Bundy of "Married with Children", the Michael Chiklis of "The Shield", the Patrick Dempsey of "Grey's Anatomy". In no time at all I will have a spin off, maybe even a starring role on a TV series or a recurring part a la Eddie on "Frasier". I won't need a speech instructor because Sprocket rarely, if ever, has any speaking parts. No, he's more of a communicator than a speaker. I'll use pantomime and charades like he does. I'm always up for non verbal communication, I find it draws people to you. It makes you seem more interesting and mysterious. Girls love quiet types and, as a herding breed, I'm nothing if not quiet.

If I Can
Make It There

12

I've gotten a new, exceedingly elegant collateral. I acquired it in preparation for my upcoming Broadway debut. Yes, Broadway. I've been thinking about my Muppet audition and, after careful contemplation of all things stuffed, I've decided that perhaps I should reconsider my career commencement vehicle. Maybe start with something geared more towards adults. Something critics will be eager to review. Something that requires daily practice to hone my skills and that will provide me with instant feedback so said skills can be honed in the right direction.

Dad says that daily training is what makes the difference between okay and great. It's what separated Master P from Jerry Rice on Dancing with the Stars. Don't get me wrong, we're not talking dancing... yet. I might take up the Paso Doble in the near future, but for now I'm going to stick with a different performing art. In any event, I trust Dad, he's never led me astray. He's led me out the door, into the car, through the weave poles... but never astray. What is *astray* anyway? I heard Dad use it the other day while telling Mom of *astray cat*. Does that mean that the cat was being led? I saw the cat as well and can assure you that it was alone. Was Dad imagining things? Did he see a nonexistent person? Should I notify the authorities? Perhaps make an anonymous call to the men with the white coats and alert them of the need of a straight jacket? I think I should just mind my business instead. I've got a lot on my mind; I don't have time to worry about what may or may not be a hallucination.

Back to Dad's daily training theory. I don't think that Mom subscribes to that belief because I constantly catch her reading magazines, not really training for anything at all—unless she's thinking of becoming a sofa cushion. She'd be perfect at that. One of the magazines that Mom reads is People—yes, apparently she's got way too much free time on her hands—here's a novel idea, Mom: Spend it with me! Or better yet, vacuum up that Golden Retriever hair—those two shed like it's nobody's business. So, if it's nobody's business, why am I telling you about it?

In any event, I was reading People over Mom's shoulder, because I lack the opposable thumbs to turn the pages myself. No, I'm not wasting my time reading the magazine, not me, I'm reading it for research. Anyway, I read that many of our best known actors got their start in theater. I believe that it's a good place for me to sharpen my teeth, uh, skills too. I'd learn a lot and get the instant audience feedback that I so crave, good and bad.

I wouldn't listen to the bad though, who wants to hear negative things about oneself? How productive can that be? But the good... ah, that would provide me with the inspiration required to perfect my craft. Through theater I could become the next Robert Redford or Hugh Jackman. I would definitely have a leg up (pardon the pun) on Hudson because he's never starred on Broadway. Between you and me, I'm not sure he has the chops for it.

I have an appointment to check out the Stella Adler acting school in Manhattan next Wednesday. This should be interesting because when I e-mailed to book my appointment, I didn't mention that I'm a dog. Some people get a little obfuscated once you tell them that you're of the canine persuasion and then they put all these limitations on you. You know what I mean, you get labeled. "He's just a dog!" they whisper when they think you're out of ear shot. I need to be able to fulfill my destiny, without the societal constraints that stifle our youth's creativity nowadays. I must have ample space to grow as a thespian. Maybe my first theater role could be as some sort of investigator, fighting crime and evil. I would be ideal for the lead role. I already know "cop" words such as "perp" and "coercion". I've even memorized people's rights when they get arrested: "You half the rice to remain silent. Anything you say Ken and Will be held again Stu..." Who the hell are Ken, Will and Stu? And what if the name of the person arrested is Brian?

I'd be a great sleuth, perhaps circa the 1940s. I could have a catchy, easy to remember, sophisticated name just like the "Pink Panther" has, perhaps I'd be known as the "Sable Shepherd". Oh, I like that, the "Sable Shepherd, Sleuth to the Stars' Dogs". I'd wear a Humphrey Bogart type hat—yikes, no! A hat would cover my ears and we can't have that, no way! I've been dying to showcase my ears to a wider audience as it is. Perhaps then I should star as a P.I. in the 1950s or 60s. I don't know... When did private eyes stop wearing hats? Once my Broadway run was up, I'd turn the script into a feature film and television series. Each week I'd solve a new mystery and have a different costarring babe or babes, three maybe. Hey, if Charlie could have three, why can't I? I'd diversify said babes, so as to reach a wider audience, one week the babes could be played by Pugs, the next Great Danes. We'd showcase a different breed with each storyline. Think of the fun we'd have.

The Web We Weave 13

I wasn't going to boast about my latest accomplishment because that's not like me. I'm more of the discreet type. No tooting my own horn, no siree Bob. Others may toot away but not I. I'm nothing if not humble. I've got so much to be boastful about, you've seen my pictures. Need I say more? Yet I keep my feet firmly on the ground... on the bed... on the wall... the muddier the feet, the better. Anyway, I was expecting Mom to send out a mass e-mail congratulating me; however, it's been a couple of weeks and she has done no such thing. Thanks Mom! Too busy to give me a little recognition, are we? People magazine taking up too much of your time again?

Unfortunately, I now find myself in the unenviable position of self promotion. Really, don't envy me, self promotion is not all it's cracked up to be. After all, who wants to hear someone drone on and on about oneself? Teeth, ears, dreams... it's exhausting I tell you! In any event, since I refuse to allow this accomplishment to go unnoticed, I will tell you myself: I passed my AKC CGC two weeks ago! (Insert congratulations, cheers and shoulder pats here.) For those of you who aren't as well versed on American Kennel Club stuff as you should be, a CGC is a Canine Good Citizen Certificate given only to those who can pass their surprisingly stringent test. It's very challenging, you can't imagine the tasks one is expected to perform. And for those of you who think it's not a big deal—back off, it's the most difficult test I've ever taken. Plus, I wasn't even 5 months old when I passed! Hello, aren't you impressed? Well, maybe if you checked your 'tude you would be. I've felt ten feet tall ever since passing the CGC. I am so proud of myself, I believe you'd say I've gotten a big head. Can you blame me? Have YOU passed the CGC? No? Perhaps then you should sheath your sword of envy and revel in my happiness.

As for my big head, it seems to be causing some issues. You see, things around me appear to be shrinking. I know it sounds preposterous but it's true I tell you. What? You don't believe me? Why would I make this up? I've been nothing but honest since I started keeping a diary and blogging in my spare time. *Blogging*, that's a funny word. It's like *logging*, but with a *buh*. I understand the word comes from "web logging". From the sound of it, it's what spiders do. Apparently, they keep logs of where they put their webs in case they should need to refresh their memory. Do spiders have so much on their minds that they need to keep notes? Really, what do they have to worry about except "fly or mosquito for dinner"?

Do they have secret lives I don't know about? Perhaps Charlotte does, what with being famous and all, but the entire spider population?

Regarding the shrinkage—not the George on Seinfeld shrinkage, I don't think that happens to my kind—the shrinkage to which I refer is environmental shrinkage. You see, I used to be able to go through Morgan's doggie door effortlessly, sadly those days are over. I now tower over said little Crested, which seems to disturb her, and am even able to look Hudson in the eye without craning my neck. Mom and Dad appear shorter too, though I've heard that humans shrink as they age. Why would they do that? I bet you that if they walked on all fours they wouldn't shrink... something to think about.

I am now larger than life. We can safely add "tall" to "fawn and handsome". One would think I'd be troubled by the shrinking of my environment, and I would be, had it more negative consequences than it seems to be having. As a matter of fact, with the exception of my inability to traverse the kitty door, I have yet to discover negative consequences. On the other hand, there seem to be quite a few positive ones to the new, smaller environment. You see, the couch, chairs, tables, kitchen counters—everything is lower, meaning that it's all conveniently within reach. Watch out casseroles here I come! As far as I'm concerned all things edible on the counter are fair game. And what fun it is to run around the house and jump on every piece of furniture in one fell sweep; it leads me to believe that I am fiercely agile. I'm going to rock the agility world, especially since I'm getting strong from all the jumping. I am strong, I am invincible, I am...

Say A Little Prayer For Me

14

October 02

It's official, the honeymoon's over. I am now in boot camp hell. Mom has started some serious training with me, unrelenting actually, all the while ranting on and on about that RN of which she spoke a few months ago. She's seemingly obsessed with it.

From what I gather, this RN is the rally novice title. She tells me not to worry about the trials—trials? Judge or jury? What did I do? This is so unfair, I haven't even spoken to a lawyer. I know my rights! What happens if I'm convicted? I've been framed I tell you, framed! Suddenly it dawns on me that Mom's probably still talking about rally, so a trial may very well be the test. Phew! I should probably check my imagination every so often. I'm sure I'll have a nightmare about this one. So, Mom says that unlike Competitive Obedience, this title is all on leash and she can speak to me throughout—you know, to remind me of what I'm expected to do, lest I should forget and go about my business at an inopportune time. She most certainly better speak to me; there is so much to remember.

In these rally trials, there are "stations" with signs to follow. These signs give instructions of actions to be executed. I don't think I'm expected to read the signs, I think Mom will do that and then she'll instruct me. I certainly hope she understands them correctly. She's been known to make a mistake or two at rally trials, just ask Desi and Hudson who each lost 10 points at one trial due to her error... yikes! Study up Mom!

Anyway, both Mom and Dad have been training me constantly. I act like I could take it or leave it but, between you and me, I live for it. You see, these training sessions are interspersed with play sessions, so much so that I sometimes get confused. Are we training or playing? This might very well be part of their evil plan—food for thought. Anyway, during these "plaining" sessions, I get tons of treats and am constantly told what a good boy I am, even when I don't do things with as much gusto as they'd like. As a matter of fact, Mom seems to become somewhat unhinged when I pretend not to hear her. The poor woman, she does all but cartwheels to get my attention. I watch her with my peripheral vision and it's all I can do not to laugh out loud at her frustration over my shenanigans. Though I pretend not to, I do learn a lot during those trying moments. I also learn a lot from Hudson. Sometimes Mom will ask me to do something and I'll go into my "this crack in the sidewalk is more interesting than you" mode, so Mom has Hudson do it and gives him my treat! Yes, MY treat! The nerve. I must give credit where credit is due though, Hudson is a fantastic worker so he does deserve my treats more than I do at times.

This home schooling really works, with some exceptions. My Afghan sister, Desi, hasn't really benefitted from it, though it could be because she's got the attention span of a newt when it comes to training. She likes playing the dumb blond (though her hair is black and tan). I guess when you're that good looking you don't need to prove how smart you are. Me, I want everyone to know I've got the brains and the looks. I want everyone to go, lalalalala, he's got the looks. (Insert Roxette music here.)

Regarding the strenuous rally training we've been doing, Mom has entered me in my first three trials—yes, already! I need to qualify in all three to get my title. They're in October which is when I am of legal AKC competition age, right at 6 months. Guess it's too much to ask to wait until I mature a bit more, is it? Just jump right in, why care about my opinion? Will I be able to handle the pressure? All three trials are outdoors; so there'll be many visual distractions and interesting aromas. I sure hope I can give Mom the attention warranted to perform the stations correctly. I shall have Hudson give me a pre-trial pep talk, you know, to build up my confidence. He got his RN at 8 months—his first trial was at six months, but then Mom couldn't find any rally trials that didn't conflict with her precious agility so a couple of months passed between trials. The trials I've entered are all before my seven-month birthday, meaning that I could beat Hudson at his own game, much like I did with the CGC. With that in mind, I believe I shall do well in Rally. Yes, first I shall conquer Rally, then the entertainment industry, then the world!

15

Guilt Trip

October 09

What a splendid day I had on Friday! I went to Manhattan. It was so exciting.!

It all started out as a guilt trip. You see, a couple of weeks ago, I inadvertently chewed one of Mom's booties to bits. The plan was just to take an innocent whiff, alas before I knew it, I was gnawing on it like it was my last meal. I didn't think anything of it but Mom and Dad were quite miffed. They didn't say anything to me as they didn't catch me in fraganti, (which begs the question, how'd they know I did it?) but I heard them talking.

I started feeling guilty and decided that I should right this wrong by replacing said booties. While they were at work, I looked at the soles and read "Manolo Blahnik". I decided to go online and order the replacement pair. Unfortunately, iPad, iMacs, and iPhones all needed passwords—really? A password on a portable device? I got news for you, Mom and Dad, if someone were to abscond with your iPhones they wouldn't return them just because they needed a password. That's right up there with a lock on a suitcase; it's an exercise in futility.

Luckily, I remembered someone mentioning that the Manolo store was in Manhattan, so I decided to trek on over and make my purchase in the flesh.

I packed a peanut butter and grape jelly sandwich, some sunglasses and a leash and off I went. It was a beautiful day. I thoroughly enjoyed the stroll on the waterfront walkway to the ferry. I didn't want to risk negotiating the trains, they're too complicated and I'd heard I could get lost in Yonkers. It was rush hour so I was able to blend in with the crowd while waiting for the ferry. Everyone was quite engrossed in their own business so I went undetected. Then the ferry docked and I noticed that people were handing the ferry guys their tickets. I didn't have one so I sidled up to the closest guy with sunglasses. Sure enough, the ferry dudes assumed I was his seeing eye dog and I boarded sans incident. I'd had the presence of mind to take a dramamine prior to leaving the house because I know the ride is four minutes, which is like two and a half hours in dog time.

I really enjoyed the ride over, the wind blowing in my face, the exhilaration of the unknown, the swaying of the ferry... back and forth... back and for—thank goodness for the dramamine.

Once in the City (that's what people in this area call Manhattan), I decided to go straight to Manolo. I found it right there on 54th street; but, it was too early and they hadn't opened yet. I thought it'd be nice to saunter through Central Park to kill some time. Good thing I had my leash with me as they don't allow dogs off leash in many parts of the park. I had a lovely time there. The trees, the people, the dogs, very relaxing. Suddenly I realized that time had slipped away and I had to rush back to Manolo and to my appointment at Stella Adler. Remember?

I quickly got back to the store and, get this, the guy that lets people in wouldn't let me in! I was percolating with fury! "That's discrimination!" I shouted, but to no avail. He wouldn't yield and kept telling me to stop barking at their door. No use hanging around. What a waste of time. So, off I went to my acting school appointment, only to find the same discrimination there. They wouldn't let me in. "I have an appointment!" I cried. They wouldn't budge. By then, I'd had all I could take and needed to clear my mind. What better way than a nice long walk...

I started walking and somehow ended up on Broadway. I believe they call it The Great White way. No, I don't know why it's not the Tiger, Mako or Hammerhead. But, Broadway is spectacular! I will definitely have to take in a play sometime. On and on I walked absorbing all the sights and odors. I was entranced. What a richness of stimuli—hot dogs, roasted nuts and French poodles on leashes!

I noticed it was getting late as my tummy started rumbling. I looked for my sandwich and it was gone. Was I the victim of a pick pocket? Perhaps I ate it absentmind-edly in frustration?

I made my way back to the ferry and got home a half hour before Dad. I washed my paws and gave myself a quick once over in the mirror, checking for tell tale signs of my adventure. Sure enough there was PB & J smeared on my mustache—false alarm on the pick pocketing. As I suspected, I'd eaten the sandwich myself. I quickly washed up and when Dad walked in I was back in my ex-pen fast asleep and he was none the wiser. Though I came back empty handed and unable to right my wrong, it was well worth the guilt trip. Why do people speak ill of guilt trips anyway? After all, I felt guilty, took the trip and no longer feel guilty. I tried to get the booties and, as they say... it's the thought that counts. I shall definitely take another trip into the City, though not a guilt trip next time. Perhaps a sight seeing trip followed by dinner and a play. I hear Godspell is coming back to Broadway.

Driving Under The Influenza

16

Ever since my adventure into the City via ferry and bus, I'd been thinking about getting a driver's license for my next guilt (or otherwise) trip. I like the idea of the freedom afforded one who can drive oneself to and fro. I also feel that I shouldn't have to travel with the masses, no offense, but really... I've heard, however, that parking can be an issue in certain places in this area. It can be impossible to find a spot or costly to pay for public parking.

Hmm, if I had someone to drive me around when Mom and Dad are otherwise engaged, you know, someone such as a chauffeur, then parking would be a non issue. But who am I kidding? Mom and Dad are in no financial position to hire one for me and I don't make enough money to pay for one myself, not yet anyway. So, I decided to get a driver's license.

First thing Saturday morning, I again packed a PB&J sandwich (my go-to staple for adventures) and some sunglasses and off I went to the Motor Vehicle Commission. I was able to walk there as all I had to do was cut through a park. It was such a lovely day and I thoroughly enjoyed it. What a lovely place. I found myself lying in the sun, coincidentally under a "no dogs off leash" sign, glancing at the geese swimming in the pond as I ate my sandwich, people watching, so relaxing... Then, I started getting looks, (probably because I'd forgotten my leash) and thought I'd better keep moving. I arrived at the MVC promptly at 11 am—I'm not a morning person so this is "promptly" for me. I'd spent more time at the park than I should have.

I was mortified to see the interminable line extending out to the street and around the corner. "Yikes!" I said to myself, "What's this?" But, I didn't answer. I stood in line for what seemed like days, though it was probably more like fifty minutes human time. While in line, I overheard several disturbing conversations, well not so much overheard as eavesdropped on them. One in particular concerned me. A gentleman was telling a lady that he had to get his license restored as it had been suspended for driving under the influenza. Let me get this straight, he's sending his license back to a store? Why? Where's the store? Can I just go buy a license there? I pondered this idea but thought it would be too much work to find out where this store was and I didn't want to risk losing my place in line after waiting so long. Thus, I decided to just stay put and get a fresh license. I also made a mental note of taking extra vitamin C when I got home and anytime I planned on driving so as not to catch the flu. I'm not sure why you'd lose your license for getting sick but I have no reason to doubt that gentleman.

Once I got called to the license issuing person behind the counter, I was somewhat thrown off by her lack of recognition of my canine persuasion. Don't get me wrong, I was pleased that I wasn't feeling the discrimination that I'd felt just last week; however, it confused me. I had prepared a speech. I was going to explain that nowhere on the MVC site does it mention that licenses are restricted to humans and that I knew I was of legal age. How did I know that? Well, as you may recall, Mom entered me in my first AKC rally trials because I turned six months old on Monday and six months is "legal age".

Anyway, the counter lady proceeded to ask me for my six-point ID verification. I was so proud of myself, I'd done my homework and knew I needed to bring verification with me. I'd made copies of my AKC registration, my pedigree form and my CGC certificate. I also took a PSE&G bill which, though in Dad's name, I thought might come in handy. I gave her the papers and, guess what? She didn't even bat an eye! Between you and me, I don't think she's getting into MENSA anytime soon.

The lady took the papers, read my name out loud and rolled her eyes. "This is your name?" she asked. "Crestview Grand Duke of Chester Gigolo? It's too long. It won't fit on the license. What do people call you?" I pointed to "Chester" and she said, "Okay, Chester Gigolo it is." There was no time to protest and I didn't want to call attention to myself, so I let it go. She asked me if I wanted to be an organ donor—*what?* I don't have any extra organs! I need the ones I have. What kind of a question is that??!!?! Preposterous!!! I looked at her in stunned disbelief and she, in turn, gave me a blank stare and checked the "no" box. She then told me to "stand there" so she could take my picture. I was looking around for a mirror and, before I knew it, flash! No time for combing my hair or opening my eyes! She didn't even ask me to say "jeez". Thank goodness the J in my PB&J was peach or I might've had it immortalized on my DL photo. Well, even though it doesn't have my full name and it's a bad picture of me, I got my license! I feel free, nay, liberated! I can now go places! I am somebody! So, the next time you're out and about, check your rear view mirror. You just might see me smiling back at you :)

No Pep Rally

17

October 23October 23

What a week! It started out a bit rough. You see, apparently I had my first AKC rally trial on Monday. I don't remember it, but that's what they tell me. No, really, I was not aware of being at any trial, I suppose that's the reason Mom was upset. She's telling everyone that I wasn't paying attention and that she actually had to excuse herself after station two, that it's the first time ever that she's had to excuse herself from a rally trial. Guess what Mom? There's a first time for everything! Valuable lessons can be learned even when one fails. You're welcome.

Anyway, all I remember is that Monday was a beautiful, windy day and that we went to a new place with dogs everywhere. I also remember that I was walked into a small, fenced-in area with signs on the ground, the grass full of goose poop, leaves flying all around, you know, lots of engaging stuff. I vaguely recall Mom's voice in the distance, could she have been talking to me? At one point, I looked at her and she seemed pleased but then—squirrel!

Moments prior to entering the ring, while sniffing around and (between you and me) blatantly ignoring Mom, she was telling Dad that my attention span was "going downhill" more quickly than Charlie Sheen can say "winning" after three lines of coke. Coke? I don't get it. Why mention soda? It was lunchtime so maybe they were planning on stopping at a drive-thru. I personally prefer Pepsi, but that's neither here nor there. And, going downhill? There were no hills, where did she see hills? This hallucinating has gotten way out of hand. Maybe it's time for professional help...

Then on the way home, I heard them saying that it would be "an uphill battle" to keep my attention in the ring. What? Again with the hills? By her tone it sounded like both comments were meant in a negative way, but how is that possible? How can downhill and uphill both be bad things? And if you live on a hill, how do you get home without traversing the negativity? Would you just have to stay home in order to avoid it? Even quit your job? Join Netflix? Order takeout and have your groceries delivered? I suppose this is a moot point if you don't live on or near a hill, or are planning on selling your hilltop home. "Moot", there's another word that has two opposite meanings. I've been thinking about this all week. It seems I can't think of anything without coming up with auto-antonyms.

Why, just yesterday I was counting my toys. I like to keep a tally lest Hudson should pilfer some. He has been known to take my stuff. Doesn't he know that all household toys are mine? Speaking of my toys, every time I get a smidgeon possessive I hear, "Chester, you need to Cher".

Listen, I like Cher just as much as the next guy, I mean, I definitely believe in life after love. However, I don't know what she has to do with my toys. Anyhow, as I overlooked them, I realized I was missing one; had I overlooked it? And if it left on its own, why were there some left? Perhaps I should clip them together? Would that secure them or separate them? Maybe I should root out the problem, then again would that remove it completely or cause it to stay permanently? Oh, em, gee!

How do people communicate anyway? It seems that verbal communication leaves a lot to be desired. My fellow quadrupeds and I have a much better system. We rarely use words, yet make ourselves understood not only to other quadrupeds but to "twopeds" as well. One look, a minuscule lip raise or even complete immobilization and a clear message is sent and received. Yes, nonverbal is definitely the way to go and, if things should turn ugly during our communication, no need to yell. We have ways of dealing with escalating conflict, too. There's nothing like a good, solid chomp to the tootsie. Words are powerful and can hurt, you say, well compare that to the seething pain of a severed toe. If you don't want to do an at-home comparison, you can ask Chicktoria, may she rest in pieces. (Ah, that's the missing toy! Now I remember.) She fell apart during one of Hudson's and my play sessions. Let's have a moment of silence for Chicktoria. A moment of silence... now that's powerful.

18

Rally On My Wayward Son

October 30

I did it! I delivered the goods. I brought home the bacon. I triumphed over the cones, though not the cones of silence. These cones were in fact silent but didn't actually silence a conversation—agent 86 would not be pleased. I was certainly pleased because I outsmarted Mom in the rally ring. She thought that I might be too young to compete and boy did I show her.

You see, before the fiasco that was my maiden trial, she'd already entered me in two other trials and, as there are no refunds after the closing date, she decided we might as well try again. "Nothing ventured, nothing gained," she said while sighing with exasperation. She seemed stressed with the fact that these two trials were also outdoors, just like the first one. We packed the car and off to the trial we went. Mom and Dad took treats and water for me, though no PB&J; those are reserved for when I go on my adventures solo.

The PB&J is an amazing culinary creation, isn't it? It's easy to prepare and packs neatly into a little sandwich baggie. What a clever invention! Think about it, a food with its own custom made home. Fascinating. Perhaps it's the packaging that makes the PB&J so intriguing to me. But I digress.

We arrived at the trial and into the ring Mom and I went. I must admit that I was a bit nervous as I didn't want to disappoint anyone again. We started our run after the judge asked, "Are you ready?" and Mom said "yes" as I cried "no". Well, as they say, if you can't beat them, join them. So, off we went and, with some occasional sniffing, successfully completed station one... station two... three... four... five... six... and then we got to seven... I'd just finished my "come forward" and was in the midst of my "finish right" when suddenly, a couple of feet from where I sat, two dogs started playing insanely and one of them let out an ear shattering, blood curdling yelp. Before I could stop myself, I ceased all forward motion and turned to look.

Mom's panic was palpable. I could even feel Dad's tense gaze on me from outside the ring, almost pleading with me. "Chester, refocus!" he seemed to yell. I tried, I really did, but I was unable. I was transfixed by their unnecessary hysteria. Those dogs were having so much fun, jumping about, barking, basking in the sunlight. Perhaps I could join them in their game. All I'd have to do was jump over the two-foot high fence that encompassed the rally ring. I was scanning the environment, planning my escape, when my eyes momentarily met Mom's for what seemed like an eternity. I expected to see a look of bitter disappointment. Instead what I saw was a look of understanding. Her eyes were telling me that it was okay to be distracted by this exhibit of recreational commotion. I was so touched by her sympathy that, at that very moment, I vowed to qualify. I pulled myself together, said "goosfraba" a few times and qualify I did! Not only did I qualify on that run, but also on my next one! I now have two of the three requisite qualifying scores toward my RN title. (To view my rally runs, both good and bad, go to: http://youtu.be/6HtH11TfFks.)

In light of my success, I've been officiously sending out resumes this week. I thought it'd be a piece of cake, however, I must say that it's been challenging at best. First, I had to learn to type sans opposables, then figure out how to print, then address envelops electronically. Dad's toys are most sophisticated and extremely complicated to use. To make matters worse, all his devices seem to be connected wirelessly. Apparently everything in the house can control the entire household. At one point, I accidentally turned the television on. Next, the ceiling fans turned on causing my resumes to fly around. How do they live like this? Why, I couldn't even turn the radio on without an instruction manual?

Finally, I went back to my envelope preparation task, alas, yet another challenge. Did you know that stamps are self adhesive nowadays? I found that out the hard way. Every time I took one off the roll it'd stick to my nose, paw, eyebrow—what was going on? Why were they sticking without being licked first? After unsticking them from their erroneous locations and before realizing their self-adhesive nature, I licked and licked, yet they seemed to get less sticky with each pass of the tongue. And don't even get me started on address labels.

Anyhow, I researched hospitals and selected some by rating, location and specialty where I might like to work. I updated my resume to add RN to my name because I anticipate getting the title at my next trial which is in the middle of November. I've already gotten responses from some of the hospitals asking for references. I've never worked anywhere so work references will be impossible to obtain. I'll have to impose upon friends for personal recommendations. The first person I'm going to e-mail is my friend Betsy in Virginia. I'm going to ask her if she'll write a letter of recommendation, you know, nurse to nurse. Wait. Nurse? Oops, much like Brittany Spears, I did it again. I confused my rally title with a nursing degree. I guess the Mayo Clinic will not be hiring me anytime soon.

Chester The Snowdog

19

November 06

I was so excited last week to see my first snowfall. Hudson tells me that I might not be as excited to see snow, come March. He says that I might tire of it—I don't think so! You should've seen the look on my face when I saw it, but no, don't hold your breath, you won't be seeing said look as there are no photographs.

Apparently the novelty that was "Chester" has pretty much worn off in the Potter household. They used to take photos and video footage of me non-stop; first bath, first new collateral, first rally trial, first sneeze, first yawn… you name it. It was like being stalked by *pup-arazzi*. I even wore sunglasses around the house for a while. Now, however, I no longer impress them with anything I do. I mean, good grief, it was my very first snowfall *ever!* And did Mom and Dad care? I guess not. Mental note: I must up my ante in order to impress these two. Meanwhile, I will try to illustrate via carefully selected words the scenario. Draw you a picture, if you will.

Imagine me sitting window-side, a tall, fawn and handsome chap. My clown-like, large nose making me even more dashing if possible. A stunning, sensational figure. Then visualize me staring out the window in bewilderment while the snowflakes were gently falling outside. A beautiful, peaceful scene. Serene even. Though, I must say that when I initially saw the white stuff dropping I was quite flummoxed. At first I though that one of the upstairs neighbors was littering, perhaps shredded kleenex? Oh, wait, it's popcorn! Popcorn! That's what was falling. Hurry, open the door! I need to get out! Someone melt some butter! I love popcorn! Mom makes it for me a few times a week. She and Dad eat most of it while I'm given only a few colonels—hmm, maybe they're not making it for me. Is the popcorn in reality for them? And why do they call them colonels? Why not captains or lieutenants? Or are there different ranks? I've only ever met colonels so I guess I assumed they were all colonels, but that wouldn't make sense, would it? Who would be in charge? If a popcorn riot broke out, it could be mass chaos.

Anyway, back to the snowfall. When Dad took me outside and I realized that it wasn't popcorn, it was all I could do not to run amuck. I loved the feel of it between my toes. Cool, soft, cushiony. It was like walking on cold chickens. It was so relaxing. Well, that was until at one point, while I was sniffing at a snowball, Dad picked it up and threw it at me! Can you believe it? Why would he do that? He didn't seem upset with me so I'm not sure what brought that on. Just out of the blue. Wham!!! It hit me right in the old kisser. Then he turned to Hudson and threw one at him. Hudson seemed prepared and caught it. The weird thing was that he almost seemed pleased that Dad had thrown it.

"Throw another one, throw another one!" he yelled. Throw another one? What is he, a masochist? So, Dad kept throwing snowballs at him and Hudson kept catching them. This family is clearly a bit off, if you know what I mean. In any event, I still enjoyed the snow experience. Unfortunately, I heard on TV that many people lost their electricity because of it. I'm not surprised. It seems that it'd be easy to lose things in the snow. I myself, picked up a rock and lost it when I dropped it in the accumulating snow, or, what's commonly referred to as a snow bank. You know, where people deposit their snow for safekeeping.

Well, I hope that now that all the snow has melted people have found their electricity. I'd be happy to help them look if they need me. I've got a fantastical sniffer you know.

20

Withering Heights

November 13

I am so proud of myself, I got my Rally Novice title this week! Yes, a *huge* congratulations to me! Can you believe it? I got the last of the three required legs on my seven-month birthday. You could say that it was a birthday present to myself. I also sang "Happy Birthday to Me, Happy Birthday to Me, Happy Birthday, dear Chester, Happy Birthday to Me!"

Why did I get myself a gift and sing to myself you ask? Well, because I needed to get something as there were no gifts otherwise... no cake... no hoopla... nothing. Didn't I tell you that the novelty that is me has worn off in our household? What more proof do you need? For those of you keeping a Chester vs. Hudson tally, I *did* beat him to the RN title! Hudson got his last leg at eight months of age. And yes, I know what you're thinking: "Did Hudson NQ at his first rally trial?" No, he did not. He got three legs in three trials. However, it is a non-issue as I plan to have my first trial expunged. I'm meeting with an attorney tomorrow morning.

Even though I am only seven months old, I already

feel grown up because I also got my official AKC agility height card this week. I guess that makes me an official agility dog. How exciting! I now measure twenty-four inches at the withers and weigh 59.6 pounds.

Speaking of withers, that reminds me of a book on my list of must reads, it's called *Withering Heights* by the well known English novelist Emily Bronte. You see, I decided that I need to include literature and music in my education in order to become a well rounded chap. Dad says it's important to be multifaceted. For those of you without a dictionary or access to the internet, ie. those of you who live under a rock, multifaceted means "many faces". I have yet to decide where to keep my extra faces. Is that something one keeps in a closet or would a bank safe be more appropriate? And why would one need more than one face? Good grief so many answerless questions. Anyway, as I cannot turn pages very efficiently, I'm going to borrow Mom's Nook to read my books. This will allow me to load them all on it and take it with me to agility trials. Agility days are soooooo long and until I can actually compete, I will have a lot of free time on my hands. Time on my hands? I don't really know what that expression means, but I heard someone using it and think it's apropos in this context. Could it be that you carry a watch in your hand? So, if pressing the buttons on the Nook proves too challenging, I will just have to listen to books on tapes. I decided which books I wanted to read mainly by what the titles tell me about them. I'd like to start with dog related books.

Here is the list so far:

Withering Heights: a book about tall dogs, perhaps taller than twenty-five inches at the withers, probably includes breeds such as Irish Wolfhounds and Borzois.

A Tail of Two Cities: about a dog that is torn between living in two cities, perhaps New York and Madrid.

The Call of the Wild: a dog receives a phone call from a wolf.

The Great Gatsby: about a Great Dane named Gatsby.

My list of classical music is:

Fur Elise: about Elise's shedding.

Fur Seasons: Winter: shedding between December and March.

Kernel Boogie March: about dancing popcorn.

Which reminds me, I haven't had popcorn in a few days; I must ask Mom to pop some for me tonight. I'd love to do popcorn and a movie. Maybe Mom and Dad are up for that. It's one of my favorite pastimes. I'd enjoy it more if we had a fireplace. I could even read my Nook fireside. I'd go through my list very quickly, though. Speaking of my list, I will begin by tackling the above-mentioned titles and expect to get through those in short order. In the meantime, I would appreciate any recommendations you might have regarding must-reads and must-hears.

21

Meet The
MACH Morgan

November 20

A *huge* congratulations to my little Crested sister Morgan on getting her MACH on Friday! As you can see from the picture, I decided it was worthy of an entry in my diary. I even posed with her for her MACH picture. You see, she needed someone to hold her humongous ribbons and, being the good sport that I am, I volunteered for the job. I didn't mind, really, I didn't. If you don't believe me, check out my expression in the picture. Anyway, by all of the fuss and believe you me there's a lot, I gather that this is something to be extraordinarily proud of. As I explained in one of my previous entries, a MACH is a Master Agility Championship title awarded by the American Kennel Club to those dogs who exhibit superior performance on the agility course. It seems to be surprisingly difficult to attain this high honor, it takes years, and is naturally more difficult for some breeds than for others. To put it in perspective roughly eight hundred Border Collies have ever gotten a MACH in the history of AKC agility, contrast that to only sixteen Chinese Cresteds, including Morgan (belonging to just ten different people, including

Mom)—yes, in the entire United States.

AKC agility began in 1994, so there have been trials for eighteen years, meaning that fewer than one Crested has received its first MACH in any given year. This stat is somewhat confusing to me. How is it possible that a dog that is less than a whole dog can run agility? What part of the dog is missing? The exteriors are all there, I know because I've seen some of those MACH Cresteds run and they look like whole dogs to me. So, it must be something inside. I even examined Morgan while she was sleeping and she seems to be a complete specimen. That's weird.

Anyway, even more impressive is the fact that out of those sixteen MACH Cresteds, only six had also gotten an AKC breed Championship, again including Morgan. She's now part of a very small, elite group of talented Cresteds. Oh, and she also has an RN. As far as we know, she is the *only* Crested to have gotten a CH, MACH and RN. My little sister is quite an inspiration to me. She still doesn't love me like I deserve to be loved but no matter, I love and admire her all the same. Yes, that's the type of guy I am. Obviously, if I had my druthers, I'd have her mentor me. However, I don't think that's in the cards; she doesn't seem amenable to the idea. But I'll tell you one thing for sure, she's got moxie, this one. How does one get moxie? I'm thinking that it's by taking "amoxiecillin". What would the correct dosage be? I'll have to ask my friend Betsy.

Speaking of Betsy, I spent a lovely day with her

yesterday at the AKC Meet the Breeds event at the Javitz Center in Manhattan. It was quite an experience for me. Mom and I drove to the ferry terminal, parked the car and purchased our tickets. I had to keep reminding myself to act somewhat bewildered by the whole experience while waiting for the ferry. I had to do that because Mom doesn't know about the first time I took the ferry into the City. Remember? She and Dad were at work and I went in for some shopping and sightseeing. Anyway, the ferry ride over was chockfull of questions, you know, "What breed is this? Do they shed? Are they obedient?", etc, etc. Once across the Hudson River, we walked to the Javitz Center where we met Bendell, Grace and Fenrir, oh, and their people too. We then spent seven hours interacting with thousands of spectators. I'm not exaggerating, there were literally thousands of them. And again with all the same questions and then some. Mom and I took it all in stride but after a few hours I excused myself for a brief respite in Gracie's crate. Then it was back to greeting more new and varied individuals who all had one thing in common; the need to fondle my ears! What is up with that? Even though I had a lovely time, by the end of my shift I was more than ready to call it a day.

Mom and I walked back to the ferry only to discover that my "shift" wasn't quite over—on the ride back to Jersey there were lots of people who hadn't gone to Meet the Breeds, but obviously should have. "What a beautiful dog. Can I pet him? What is he?"...

Giving Thanks 22

It's official, I love Thanksgiving. I don't know much about holidays. As a matter of fact, I don't know much about history, don't know much biology, don't know much about a science book and I've never taken French. But a holiday in which all you do is eat, wow, who would've thought?

Mental note: find French tutor as soon as possible. I must get back to my roots. Maybe I'll go to Berlitz instead. I understand they have a solid, reputable learning system. I could learn enough to socialize with my relatives when I go to France and perhaps even figure out what "Foux du Fafa" means. That reminds me that I need to get my passport, maybe next week. But I digress.

Turkey day is the first big holiday of my life, making it all the more special. Though one could argue that the Fourth of July is just as major a holiday. I was a little too young at the time to appreciate that one, though. Plus, it's more of a drinking than an eating holiday and I'm a teetotaler at heart. I think Thanksgiving would've been better were Mom and Dad not vegetarians—I mean really, no turkey on Thanksgiving? What sort of weirdos are they? No meat? Don't get me wrong, my siblings and I eat meat, however, Mom and Dad don't. And what do I care, you ask? Why judge? To each his own, you say? Well, normally I'd agree, but this is inconvenient because it directly affects my dietary intake. Case in point, nearly three hundred million turkeys sacrifice their lives each year in the U.S. for Thanksgiving. Three hundred million and I couldn't get one? Just one?!? So Mom and Dad are vegetarians, so what! They couldn't buy a turkey and let the rest of us eat it? I would've been happy to share it with Hudson and the girls, provided there was some sort of sweet potato dish as well.

I've never actually tasted turkey, however they look like overgrown chickens to me and I like me a good piece of chicken. Plus, they're so big that we could've had left-overs, which I hear are tastier than the source. Heck, I would've even been happy with a Canadian goose. I could've caught it myself; they're everywhere in our neighborhood.

Mom told me that, besides eating, I had to take some time to thank God for all His blessings. To that end, I made a list: I am thankful for my family, friends, health, kibble, treats, Picardness, looks, personality, wit, talent, IQ and, most of all, for not being a turkey. I don't think turkeys have anything to be thankful for on Thanksgiving. What kind of a life is that of a turkey? I'm not going to get into it. Let's just have a moment of silence for the poor gobblers.

Anyway, it would seem that I am fascinated by major holidays. I hear that this Christmas one is a real doozy, too. It obviously must be because Dad had us all dress up for the Christmas photo. Apparently my family makes a Christmas card every year. See what I mean? Weirdos. I'm not going to tell you what he made us wear because it's somewhat embarrassing and I don't want to relive it, you'll just have to see it for yourself.

Deck The Howls

23

Yet another eventful day chez Chester. Today, we decorated the house with lights and trinkets. My first Christmas and I was allowed to help with the decorations. Well, not as allowed as I would've liked, however I did help. Okay, not so much help either. Let's just call it "participate". From the pictures I've seen of last year's tree, this year's is smaller and they placed it atop a table. Mom says they did this to be different from other years, but I know that it's because they're trying to keep it out of my reach—yeah right! Don't they know that nothing in my home is out of my reach? You'd think they would've figured that out by now.

In the few hours that we've had the Christmas stuff out, I've heard "leave it" three million two hundred and eleven thousand times. I comply every time, then proceed to pick up the next bauble in my line of sight and act stunned when asked to leave that too. I know they mean that I need to leave everything, but I'm just trying to get my bearings and familiarize myself with this holiday. As you can imagine, I was very curious when Dad brought some boxes marked "Christmas Stuff" up from the garage. No sooner were these Christmas boxes open, that I tried to pick something up. Where to begin? So much stuff, I almost didn't know what to reach for next. And get this, to add to the excitement, Dad was eating popcorn and shared some with me! You know how I like my popcorn!

I've heard that you can make popcorn decorations. I believe you sew it together and make a garland of sorts. I'm not sure how I feel about this. On the one hand, popcorn is for eating and should not be played with nor turned into a knickknack and wasted on a tree. On the other hand, is it really wasting? After all, I could eat it once the festivities are over making cleanup easier for everyone.

Anyway, it was all fun and games today until Mom decided it would be amusing to decorate me. Yes, me! She actually put this jingle-belled collar on me! Every time I moved it made noise. Obviously, I wasn't having any of that, no possibility of going undetected with that on. A large part of my stealthiness comes from my ability to move silently across the floor. So, I gave Mom this pathetic look and voila! Off with the collar! I must say that I've got that look down to a science. I use it for all my needs; go out, food, water, play...all of it. Back to the tchotchkes, everything looks so pretty. I especially love the lights on the tree. Do you hear what I'm saying? There's a tree IN the house! Or as I call it, a bathroom in the living room. Now that I think about it, the lights and ornaments they put on it present somewhat of an inconvenience to me. Perhaps I'll just admire this one while I continue "conducting my business" on the trees outside.

Allons-y!

24

December 11

Yet another adventure for yours truly. As you know, I've been meaning to get my passport so I can plan a trip to the motherland. I've also looked up French tutors and, once I gather the necessary funds, will start lessons. There are two ways to get your passport, you can either mail in the requisite paperwork or go to an office in person. If I mailed the paperwork, I'd have a difficult time explaining to Mom and Dad how I got my passport when it arrived. They don't approve of my independence at such a young age. Plus, going into an office in person would give me a reason for a long overdue adventure.

I googled a passport office and located one on Hudson street in the City. My brother Hudson was so excited when I told him the address that he asked if he could tag along to keep me company. Between you and me, I think he just wanted to get a picture under the street sign. You know, Hudson on Hudson. Unfortunately, I had to decline this most generous offer. You see, Hudson is a little too friendly and is easily distracted by—squirrel! Get it? So, I got up early, waited for the folks to leave for work and packed up. PB&J... check. Freshly popped popcorn, please hold the butter... check. Banana... check. Bottled water... check. Waterway ferry, here I come.

I enjoying traveling on the ferry. I make many friends on that short ride and I've really gotten the hang of it. Once on the east side of the river, I boarded a bus and headed to the passport office. The map I printed proved most helpful and I quickly found the office. Getting a passport was more difficult than I'd thought it'd be. The guy I went up to at the counter gave me a once over and excused himself. He whispered something to a co-worker assuming that I wouldn't hear. Hello, dude, have you seen the size of my ears?

He was talking about my beard and mustache and the fact that he needed to check the "Error-ist Watch list". Is that a list of people who incorrectly watch something on television because they don't know how to use their re-mote control? Or is it people who mis-program their DVR rendering them unable to watch the desired show? Either way, lacking a basic knowledge of electronics should not be a punishable offense. Why are those people unworthy of passports? Are we to assume they'd be unable to plan a trip? If you ask me, that's profiling. A guy should be able to sport facial hair without being judged.

I'm happy to say that in the end I was successful in obtaining a passport, yay me! I thought it'd take longer than it did, so I found myself with a bit of extra time on my hands. I'd heard of the Rockefeller Center Christmas tree and decided I'd go take a look-see. And take a look-see I did! Oh my gosh! It's fantastic! So much surface area for... well, you know what. Then, I saw the ice skaters. Hmm, that looked like fun. I was torn between giving it a go or traipsing over to the Empire State Building. I can see it from home and have been thinking about going for quite some time. The ESB won, not in small part because I also wanted to see the window displays at Macy's which are on the way. They're spectacular! I highly recommend you see them. I then crossed the street and, to my surprise, the line to go up the ESB was out the door. Yikes! I knew I couldn't stay and make my ferry. The ESB would have to wait. I got home in time to get back into my crate undetected. As I lay there and looked at our itsy bitsy, miniature, pathetic Christmas tree, I couldn't help but feel like Charlie Brown. Then I realized that the spirit of Christmas lies within us, not within the size of a tree. And, much like the Grinch, my heart grew three sizes that day.

Yes Chester, There Is A Santa Claus

25

December 18

What a wonderful season this is. Okay, with the exception of getting shot on Friday, it's a wonderful season. Mom tells me not to be dramatic. She says that I wasn't shot. She says that what the vet did was give me a rabies vaccine, but I was shot nonetheless and *ouch!*

Anyway, I am so excited to learn more about all things Christmas. This week, Dad told me that I needed to write to Santa Claus with my Christmas list. My first question was, "who is this Santa fellow?" Well, I didn't actually ask him because I didn't want to appear uninformed, so I waited until I could get my paws on a computer and Googled it. OMG, this guy is one cool dude! Did you know that he not only answers letters, but that, in most cases, he also gets you what you ask for? Well, that's provided you ask for reasonable things and not for two first class tickets and luxury accommodations to Paris—learned that the hard way. He himself travels by sleigh, which seems somewhat old fashioned; yet it's pulled by flying reindeer, which is definitely futuristic. I don't get it, I've seen deer and believe you me, they don't fly. Though

I must admit that I've never seen any of the "rein" persuasion, maybe those do, in fact, fly. I understand that you can now even Skype with Santa. Wow, he must be so busy this time of year what with gifts, letters, travel, etc. I haven't tried Skyping with him because we've recently gotten antlers to chew on and I don't want Santa, Dasher, Dancer, Prancer, Vixen, Comet, Cupid, Donner, Blitzen or Rudolph to see them and get offended. Worse yet, they could get scared and skip our home altogether come gift delivery time. They may not know that these antlers are collected from the ground. Apparently, in most arctic and temperate-zone areas, deer shed their antlers regularly. So no need to panic, no animals were harmed in the making of my chew toys.

In any event, I made my Christmas list and mailed it via U.S. Postal Service to Santa. I only asked for a handful of things because I don't want to appear greedy and start off on a bad note with the guy. I asked for a new collateral, a month-long public transportation pass, a few stuffed toys for me as well as some to share with my siblings, and a couple of gift certificates for Mom and Dad to their favorite stores. I would like the transportation pass to include both the ferry for my City adventures and all buses. I need buses to be included in my travel pass because I've recently "met" a young lady whom I'd like to get to know better. I've seen her in pictures and received a couple of e-mails from her. Her name is Gita and she's got long, sexy legs and an engaging expression. I'm sure she's also got a mysterious accent as she's from the former Eastern Bloc, the Czech Republic to be exact. I've got to Google that too so I can impress her. I have it all planned, I'll have Mom give me a bath the day before my trip. How? Well, as you might have gathered, I'm quite resourceful. All I have to do is roll in mud or something smelly and voila! Immediate bath. I'll pack a sandwich, banana, and popcorn and will wear my new collateral. I'll also wrap one of the new toys, then take an early bus upstate. I will arrive at her doorstep, present her with the gift and proceed to woo her with my knowledge of all things Bohemian. I might even put "Bohemian Rhapsody" on my iPhone and play it as background music when I ring the doorbell and wait for her to open the door; that's sure to make an impression. If things work out, I'll have to help her get a passport too so that we may combine my France trip with one to her native land. I've got to admit that I'm a bit wary of making plans with Gita because her mom is somewhat of a worry wort. You see, I was originally supposed to meet Gita last month but there was a rumored flu going around and her mom didn't let her socialize with anyone. I guess fate had other plans for us and perhaps meeting each other once Gita is more mature is a better idea.

C Is For Canine

Merry Christmas! ¡Feliz Navidad! Joyeux Noël! Frohe Weihnachten! Buon Natale! No matter in what language, I hope it's a very happy day for you and yours. Don't forget to wish baby Jesus a happy birthday as you open a Christmas present, after all, isn't that what this season is really all about? Stay safe, don't overeat (I know I will), and may God bless you with everything you wish for and more. I know that He has blessed me on this, my first Christmas, which has been quite an enlightening season. Not only have I started learning to speak different languages, as evidenced above, but I've also become acquainted with the fat, uh, I mean the horizontally challenged, bearded gentleman and his reindeer... not to mention their tasty antlers. I've experienced the joy of giving and the even greater joy of receiving. I've taken up yoga and learned to meditate. I've even contemplated my future and decided that, given my ease of learning, particularly languages, I should seriously consider a career in espionage.

I've been watching a lot of Bond films lately and have

realized that I possess all the qualities needed by a spy; I'm dashing, debonair, intelligent, stealthy and observant. Think about it, I can combine those qualities with my love of travel and ease of meeting people. Have passport, will travel. I should probably start with some on-the-job-training in a less hazardous field so as to perfect my craft. Yes, I shall find a job as a Private I. Or is it Private Me? Anyway, I'll travel the United States and solve dastardly crimes, such as "Man Disappears in Virginia Cave While Spelunking". Why a person would rappel into a cave is beyond me, however I'm not one to judge. To each his own, I say. But back to the Christmas season.

We had a lovely Christmas Eve. Mom, Dad, grandma and I walked three miles round trip to a Target store. There were so many people everywhere. Santa hats galore. Cars driving by with red noses and antlers...? Oh boy, I'd never been so excited, so many different things to stimulate one's senses. Everyone fawned all over me as we meandered around the shops. I thoroughly enjoyed the attention. What I didn't enjoy, however, was when Dad and I had to stay outside the store while Mom and grandma went in. I would've loved to have gone in and checked it all out. How am I to sharpen my investigatory skills if I'm not permitted to examine new environments up close and personal? Unfortunately, I was thwarted in my efforts by an absurd "no dogs allowed" sign. Who's the Einstein that came up with that bright idea? What heartless eggnog of a man, or woman, invented that silly rule? Maybe those who don't love dogs should be the ones waiting curbside? What a sad life is that not shared with a dog. Maybe Santa can do something about it. On the walk back home, we stopped at a Starbucks and sat outside to drink lattes. The temperature was an invigorating 40 degrees with a bright, warm sun to make it just perfect. It was even more enjoyable because Mom let me chew on her Starbucks coffee splash stick. It tasted of Gingerbread latte. I gave Mom the "can I have a latte too or at least share some of yours?" look to no avail, so I had to settle for gnawing on the stick. Again I digress.

I've started researching different venues of employment so as to apply for a spy job once I've sharpened my skills. Perhaps the CIA? The more I write about this, the more excited I get! Oh, now that I think of it, I must buy some hats and cigarettes. I don't intend on taking up smoking but I've seen many an investigator with a cigarette hanging out of his mouth. As you may recall, I've always had a penchant for crime solving but to become the James Bond of the canine world... wow! Excuse me, aren't you—? Gigolo, Chester Gigolo. Double O seven-C.

Happy New Year! Yet another holiday about which to learn. Not only that, but this new year thing is a phenomenon that perplexes me. If we were doing okay with 2011, then why get rid of it? On the other hand, if we weren't, why not keep it and try to improve on it? If at first you don't succeed, try and try again I say. Don't throw in the towel. The ball yes, but the towel no. There's no fun in retrieving a towel. I'll be sad to see 2011 go, this has been an important year for me.

Think about it, this is the year in which I was born, in which I moved, learned how to swim, meditate, lost and found my teeth, became a chef, discovered feature films, got my nursing degree, obtained a driver's license and a passport, and quietly sat in my siblings' shadows during their moments of success. Plus, now that I've gotten used to writing 2011, I'll have to get used to writing 2012 instead. That's going to take some time and a lot of ripped up checks, I'm sure. I'll certainly adapt. I've had to adapt to a lot in my short, albeit productive, life, so far. The biggest change of all was my adoption. The fact that I'm still meeting family members sometimes presents a challenge as well. As I told you last week, grandma is here visiting. She's my maternal grandma. Apparently, she lives in Spain. Google maps tells me that it's near France. Perhaps I'll go there on my France trip and turn it into a European vacation. I'll be the Chevy Chase of the canine world. Anyhow, it pains me to say that grandma is not a dog lover. I know, it was a shock to my system too. You see, I've always been surrounded by friends and family who love me or strangers who admire me. Meeting someone, especially a family member, who is not automatically impressed by me has been an unpleasant experience. Grandma does have many words of praise for me. She says I'm beautiful, intelligent, well behaved and obedient. Yet, when I try to engage her in play, she gives me the "you've got to be kidding me" look and then proceeds to ignore me. Ignore *me?* What?!? Mom tells me not to take it personally, that not everyone is a dog person. Not a dog person? I don't even know what that means.

What's worse is that grandma seems more than willing to walk my fourteen and a half year old sister Kelly and does so regularly. Hmm, what's so special about her? She's a Golden Retriever for the love of guacamole. They're a dime a dozen. As previously mentioned, Kelly is my brother Hudson's biological grandmother. Yet both he and she are my siblings. Oh my, it's too confusing even for me. Let's just leave it at Kelly's my sister, Hudson's my brother and Luz is our grandmother. Well, due to grandma's lack of interest in playing with me, I've decided that I shan't visit her on my trip to Spain.

But back to the new year celebration. We celebrated at home because Dad didn't want us to drive anywhere. He said that it's not safe to be on the road on new year's eve. He tells me that there were most likely a lot of driving under the influenza summonses issued because of the celebratory habits of many people. There seems to be quite a bit of drinking involved in these festivities, which leads me to believe that drinking causes the flu. Me, I'm a tee totaler so I won't be needing a flu shot.

Our new year's celebration involved eating twelve grapes and drinking champagne. The grapes are a custom from Spain, they're eaten at the rate of one per second, on the twelve seconds prior to ringing in the new year. Each grape represents a month of the year. It brings good luck to finish your grapes before the new year bells ring, but it brings bad luck to choke on one because you're eating them without chewing. In any event, it wasn't an issue for us kids as we were not allowed to partake in said custom because "leave it, grapes aren't good for dogs!" We were given twelve bits of kibble instead—yippee. They gave us twelve pieces of the same dog food we eat everyday, how generous. Speaking of generosity, may the spelling gods grant you the ability to write 2012 without having to think about it. In case they're not feeling particularly generous with me, I'd better go practice writing 2012, 2012, 2012...

Frisbee Mania

Frisbees. Who invented frisbees? Whoever did so should be knighted. Or dayed; or whatever.

What's so great about the 'sbees? Well, if you have to ask, you've clearly never played with one. What could be greater than a flying circle of fun? I so enjoy chasing them and highly recommend you give them a shot. Well, don't actually shoot them, we're not talking skeet here. I believe those 'sbees are made of clay. Pull!

I suggest you play the way Mom and I do. She throws them for me almost every morning and I catch the ones that stay up in the air long enough. It's challenging because Mom doesn't throw them very well, so sometimes they're up in the air for all of a nanosecond. What can I say? No matter how proficient a guy is at catching an object mid-flight, there's no catching those. Those I pick up off the ground and run them back to Mom so she'll throw them again. I wish we could play for hours, but Mom tires long before I do. I must admit that I've gotten really good at multitasking. I have to keep my eyes on the frisbee, while at the same time looking ahead, so I don't run into anything. After all, who wants to body slam a goose and get a mouthful of feathers? Plus those guys aren't as friendly as you might think, and if frightened, they'd most likely attack. That'd be an ugly fight which I'd probably win, though there's no telling because they tend to gang up on one.

Mom says that a group of five geese is called a gaggle. I'd never heard that word before so I had to look it up. The internet explains that a gaggle is eight fifty-pound bags of salt. So it would seem that five geese are made up of four hundred pounds of salt. Due to this, I've come up with a fantastic idea. I've started rounding geese up and keeping them in a small area outside the apartment. Every morning I re-group my geese into a tight little circle and count them—which is not the same as counting your chickens before they hatch. I plan on keeping them there and awaiting a snowstorm. I will then sell them to the highest bidder to pulverize. I can't do it myself because I lack the necessary equipment. What would one use to pulverize geese?

Anyway, once in crystalline form they can be sprinkled onto roadways to melt ice so cars get a better grip. This will also help control goose overpopulation. It's a win-win situation, though I'm sure said geese would beg to differ. Speaking of win-win, I snuck out of the house again today. This time I made it to a Whole Foods grocery store. That's where Mom and Dad get their groceries so I thought I could find something more exciting for us kids to eat. Anything sounds more exciting than our usual kibble. All I can say about that place is wow! Like I said, win-win. I went on an adventure *and* ate like a king. I sampled everything, everything! That is, of course, until I was "invited" to leave. Some nimrod started with the "no dogs allowed" garbage, there was a small scuffle, and voila! Off with their heads! Yes, a few people lost their heads. Or is the expression lost their minds? In any event, I was escorted out in a most humiliating way, with a bottle of Hint water in my paw, mouth full of nacho chips, and organic salsa on my mustachio. I made the mistake of going sans disguise today, big mistake... huge. Next time I must pull out the sunglasses, hat, and trench coat.

Well, I went into the city again on Friday. This wasn't one of my notorious PB&J adventures, no sir. This time I went in with Mom, Dad and grandma. Actually, Hudson and Morgan were there too. It was so cold and windy. That Manhattan is like one huge wind tunnel. My hair was flying all over the place, I had to stop three times to comb it. I should've worn a coat and hat because it was as cold as it's ever been, I think I even saw snow. What I know I saw were some people camping out on 49th Street to see Daniel Radcliff. At first I thought they were there for me, then I realized that they were unfazed as I walked by and they glanced over. I must admit that I was confused by the fact that they seemed completely unimpressed by my presence. Well, not completely, they did fawn over me once they made eye contact. Wait a minute! It just dawned on me that I'm fawn in color and that people fawn over me. Coincidence? I think not!

Why were we in the city, you ask? You see, the three of us were hired to work on Saturday Night Live. I wonder why they call it live? Is there a dead version I don't know about?

It was my first time walking around the city with my folks, first time going into the NBC studios, and first time working with eight other dogs, six of whom were strangers! A trifecta of firsts, if you will.

We had to go up to the studio in a freight elevator. That was only my second time in an elevator, the first was at the Javits Center. The Javits elevator was small so I knew that something was up... or down, depending on where you're going. The NBC elevator is huge so I thought we were all walking into a "little room" for some sort of clandestine canine meeting. You know, to discuss important topics such as: to bite or not to bite, running away, should one dig out or sprint through an open door, when crate use gets out of hand, and other such topics. Imagine my surprise when the room started moving. I stayed cool and pretended not to notice. The Greyhounds, on the other hand, looked a bit panic-stricken. Besides my Golden and Crested siblings, there was a Shih Tzu, Old English Sheepdog, Irish Setter, Scottish Terrier, and two Greyhounds.

My thoughts on the dogs? The Shih Tzu... well, who would want to go through life with that answer to "what breed are you"? The Greyhounds were spitting images of my Afghan sister Desi on a bad hair day. They could be used as the "before" image and Desi as the "after" in a Hair Club for Dogs ad. The OES reminded me of an over-stuffed pillow. At one point I even laid my head against it and started to fall asleep until Mom gave me a dirty look. The Irish Setter resembled an undernourished, sun-burned Golden Retriever with low set, houndy ears. The Scotty looked very distinguished, almost like looking in one of those fun house mirrors.

We filmed a pre-taped skit for the live show. Hudson and I had to sit by the Sheepdog and Setter, then interact with them and eat some food off the table. To Dad's horror, the Setter was in season. I found her scent intoxicating and had a bit of trouble concentrating. Hudson seemed unfazed and able to work, but then he's almost three years old and a seasoned actor. Me, I'm only nine months old. I'm still a baby though it might not seem like it because I weigh sixty-five pounds, measure twenty-five inches at the withers and am twenty-seven inches shoulder to buttock—I know this because Mom measured me the other day; I'm not sure why.

My point is that at nine months of age I did a heck of a fantastic job in that environment. I also socialized with a million people at the studios, all of whom asked what breed I was. It was almost embarrassing that so many people singled me out in a group of dogs to say how "adorable, beautiful, sweet, well behaved..." I was. I felt somewhat guilty that none of the others was the target of public admiration.

Before this weekend, I'd never watched SNL because

I'm an early riser and it's on well after my bedtime. I enjoyed the show, however, and would have become a steadfast fan. Unfortunately, despite my stellar performance, my segment was not used. They only used a millisecond of the pre-tape. The millisecond consisted of the Shih-Tzu sitting at a table and one can barely tell what one is looking at because of the duration of the clip. Most upsetting. I really thought that my salubrious lifestyle would lead to instant stardom. Alas, said stardom is not as forthcoming as one would hope; however I will not allow this bitter disappointment to discourage me in my quest for fame—this I vow!

Gambles With Wolves

30

Yet another exciting adventure for Chesterton! This time I took the bus south. I'd always heard the term "southern hospitality" and wanted to experience it for myself. What better way than a trip down south to the Atlantic City casinos? (Between you and me, I didn't think they were all that hospitable.) Anyway, the casino idea came to me because I thought I might enjoy winning some extra cash. I even made a shopping list. It consisted of typical things a chap such as I would need: a tux, microwave popcorn, a new scarf and three gloves. Only three because I need to keep my other paw free in order to use my iGadgets. Alas, winning was not meant to be.

Early Tuesday morning, I packed a PB&J, sunglasses and overcoat and made my way to the bus. I had some trouble boarding it because I needed to sidle up to a sunglass-wearing passenger so as to reprise my seeing-eye dog gig. Easy, right? Wrong! It was raining so only yours truly donned sunglasses. Luckily the bus driver got momentarily distracted and I was able to board unnoticed. It's getting more and more challenging to go unnoticed, undoubtedly because of my rugged good looks.

Once in A.C., I tried my hand at everything—slots, black jack, roulette and craps. Something to keep in mind about the craps table... that's not what it's for. I know, I know, it's green and plush like grass, what's a fellow to think? It's beckoning to be used. And use it I did. That's when I was rudely escorted out the nearest door. But, I didn't really care because in those seventeen minutes I'd spent gambling, I lost all my cash.

Disappointed, I returned to the bus station to make my way home to the northern country. On the ride back, I wondered why in the world anyone would get involved in gambling. Then it hit me! I was on the wrong end of the leash, so to speak. I needn't play *against* the casino, I needed to BE the casino!

I got home and ran to the computer. After much research, I discovered that the fastest route to casino ownership, besides hitting the lottery, is to become a Native American. I didn't think that was an option for me, so I popped some corn, lightly buttered it and sat on the couch to watch an episode of "I Dream of Jeannie". I enjoy it because Dad's a former military pilot, he's also a major like Major Nelson. Watching the show is like looking in a window to Dad's past life. Did he find Mom on a beach? Was Mom a beached whale? Coincidentally, this episode was the one in which Jeannie is curious about her past. That's it! I would go on www.canineancestry.com

and research my "Jeannieology".

A few hours later, I found it. I'm actually 1/225th Mohegan. That's so obvious, how could I have missed it? Mohegan means wolf! If I had to pick a tribe, it would've been this one. The Mohegan Sun casino is just next door in Connecticut. I shall petition the tribal council to become a member of their tribe.

Did you know that their members receive four out of every ten dollars gambled? Imagine my shopping list then. I could go on many adventures with that kind of dough. Better yet, I could even bake some bread with it, probably croissants, a nod to my French heritage. I'd really like to invent the "whole wheat " croissant, do they exist? I could open a Native American/French fusion cuisine restaurant in the City. My dishes would have exotic names such as "Falling Rain Leek Pie", "Wigwam Camembert" or "Dewdrop Crepes". The food would be organic, vegetarian *and* low in sodium, fat and calories. I'd call it "Le Chien Amerindien". Michelin would undoubtedly rate it three stars. It would be off the charts in Zagat. I'm hungry just thinking about it. Is there any blueberry jelly left?

Basic Instinct

January 29

This week's diary almost went unwritten. Stop panicking and pull yourself together—I said "almost". I was too upset to write but then decided I mustn't let Mom's inappropriate question get the better of me. You see, Mom and I were sitting on the sofa, eating popcorn side by side, watching TV as per "yuge". We were having a lovely time, when, during a commercial break, Mom glanced over and asked "Chester, what look are you going for with that hair?"

Yes, she actually asked that! The worst part is that she was serious. Can you believe it? A chap's entitled to sport any look he wants, however unconventional. If I want tousled hair, who's to say that it's frumpy? Hey, it works for me. I get many admiring glances from the ladies. And "by the way, Mom, if you have to ask about my style, I'm not explaining", I said. Well, I didn't really say it but my eyes spoke volumes as I stared at her. I could tell she'd heard me loud and clear as I jumped off the sofa and she mumbled, "teenagers!"

Mom and Dad have been in a foul mood as of late.

Perhaps it's because of Hudson's and my incessant whining over Desi and Morgan. Is it our fault that both girls are in season? What choice do we have but to whine? They won't let us near them and yet we're forced to breathe the same air that they do. We can't help it, it's instinct so no matter how many times you ask us to be quiet, the whining is not going to stop. Maybe my folks need to read up on "instinct".

Unfortunately, they're not the only ones who need to read up on it. I mean really, how many of us haven't heard, "they're not aggressive, that's just the way they were raised," when speaking of a certain other breed? I'm referring to the breed responsible for forty percent of dog related human fatalities in this country. I'm not going to mention the breed because I don't want to ruffle anyone's feathers. Think about it, some of us have the instinct to herd, some to retrieve, some to kill. You don't breed in a trait for two hundred years and then blame it on "how they were raised". Come on, use your noggins people! You can only control instinct for so long, sooner or later it rears it's ugly head.

Case in point, Mom decided we needed to repaint our living room, dining room, kitchen and hallway. Mom's color of choice was yellow. Yellow? Good grief woman, what's wrong with you? Now it looks like we live on the sun! I have to wear sunglasses from the moment I wake up in the morning, even if it's raining outside. Anyway, no sooner had Mom and Dad started painting the living room that, as is my instinct, I sprung into action to help them. For some reason, my help was unwanted. I picked up a brush, it was taken from me. I picked up a roller, taken as well. Next up, the plastic floor protection... and that's when I got barricaded in the kitchen. Like I said, instinct is a powerful thing, if you don't want the help of a herding breed, get another Afghan Hound. Just kidding Desi, though we both know that you wouldn't lift a paw to help Mom and Dad unless they were being chased by a pack of wild hare. How does a person get chased by hare anyway? Is it a pony tail gone mad in the wind? Wouldn't simply taking scissors to it solve that problem? Now back to ruffling feathers, in case you're wondering, my pulverized geese business was a bust. Not only was I unable to find a buyer, but I also got laughed out many a door. Is the conventional method of obtaining salt really better or am I just ahead of my time?

February 5

I lost my Afghan sister Desi this week; she passed away on Wednesday quickly and unexpectedly; we don't know why. Maybe her heart? She would've been 10 years old tomorrow. There's been so much sadness at home lately and, though Desi and I didn't play together, I've found myself a bit weepy as well. I miss her. Please remember her in your prayers tonight.

She was a beautiful, elegant girl. Mom and Dad have always said that I was like her in many ways: my agileness, my build, my occasional aloofness, and even my elegance. I've been thinking a lot about her, especially this weekend. You see, our winter break is over and it's back to the agility grind, along with the lengthy car rides. Desi and I used to love looking out the windows together. Now I'm left to enjoy the view all by me onesies... Only my Crested sister Morgan and Golden brother Hudson compete at the moment. I hope to start late this summer. Yikes! Will I be ready? Will I get the crazies and run amuck like Desi occasionally did to Mom's pleading cries of "Come. Come here now!!"?

I do show promise, though. We went to practice in a life size, fully stocked agility ring for the first time this week. To even my amazement, I did quite well. I did mini sequences and was able to negotiate all the obstacles, except for the weaves and tunnels. In my defense, I wasn't asked to take the weaves because I'm too young still. However, the tunnel was another story. Try as hard as they may, Mom and Dad could not convince me that it was safe. It was dark and small. I'd most certainly bump my head against the top. What if I hurt my ears? I refused to go in, refused! Discussion over! They didn't compel me so I assumed I'd won that battle.

Lo and behold, we got home and Dad brought a scrunched up tunnel into our living room—he's deranged I tell you! He asked me to go in but I was having none of that no matter how short it was. Again with the tunnel? Didn't we already agree to disagree? Undaunted, Dad turned to Hudson and asked him to go in. In he went and came out the other end, happy as a clam. Hmm, I'd clearly created much ado about nothing. Maybe I'd try it just once, but it had to be my idea. I couldn't have Dad believe that I'd relented.

"Okay", I said, "I want to try it now," and in I went. "Wee, this is cool," I thought. Then, I went in again and again. I thought I was imagining things as it seemed to take longer to get through it each time. Then I realized that Dad was actually making it longer. By the end of our session it was full length, yet I still enjoyed it. It was almost as much fun as this thing called an A-frame. I negotiated that obstacle the first chance I got, climbing it with ease. I'm not sure if I enjoyed the obstacle as much as the awestruck look on Mom's face at my eagerness to take it. I think I'm really going to have fun with this agility thing. Bring on the boot camp!

Speaking of enjoying, I can't wait for the Super Bowl. I've been hearing a lot of buzz and am anticipating it anxiously. I don't know much about it, though. I've got many unanswered questions even after my endless snooping. What does a cartoon Beagle have to do with curiosity? Anyway, first time I heard about the Super Bowl was the folks talking about it. The more they spoke, the more I hung on every word—this is rare for me; I don't normally care much about what they're saying. Pry as I might, I was unable to find out where this Super Bowl is. I know it'll be on today, but, on what? Dining room table? Kitchen counter? Who's putting it there? And what exactly is going to be in this large bowl? Something edible I hope. I've prepared a fork and spoon along with some milk so I am ready for any eventuality.

I had a minor break in the case today. Dad told Mom that the Super Bowl will be on NBC. They're very wily these two, speaking in code, thereby making my discovery mission more difficult. NBC. Near the Big Chair? That narrows it down to the master bedroom and the living room. I have positioned myself in the hallway so as to better observe both rooms. I've been staking them out all day, to no avail. I don't know how much longer I'm going to wait. I'm losing interest. Maybe I'll just go make myself a PBJ and see what's on the tube.

Hudson Goes Live – Grrr!

33

Does anyone know the laws governing legal work age for canines? Is it older than 10 months? If so, does anyone know of a good attorney? I only ask because I've been working non-stop. I filmed a phone company commercial last week in which I had a lot of action scenes, and, yes, I even had to do my own stunts. No stunt doubles were hired and, quite frankly, I don't think they could've done as good a job as I did. (Insert back pats here.) Everyone was very friendly and I really enjoyed the treats and attention.

Then this week, I had to pose with some children for a Company Kids catalog shoot. I'd met some of the staff before and it was nice to see them again. Last time they saw me was when they put me on the cover of their winter 2011 catalog; I was only two months old at the time. I think this shoot was for the cover of the spring 2012 catalog. They were all surprised at how big I'd gotten and, though it was a lovely shoot, I did have a beef with my fellow actors and some advice for casting directors: when hiring kids to work with canines, why not ensure that said munchkins are amenable to canines? I mean, really, kids that are weary of standing within a few feet of a sitting dog? Maybe these kids need some training. I'm just saying.

As is patently obvious, I'm in a somewhat negative mood today. It could be because I've got a bone to pick with Hudson. Yes, my brother, my best friend, my mentor, has stepped over the line. I hope I can get over it, but it's not going to be easy.

As you may recall, Morgan, Hudson and I all did a pre-taped segment for Saturday Night Live a few weeks ago, in which I did a bang up job, even if I do say so myself. Then our segment was cut. Well, Mom explained that this happens all the time and that it was nothing personal. I never gave it a second thought until Friday, when Hudson got hired to work on SNL again, though this time without yours truly. I stayed home with Dad and settled in to watch the show yesterday, you know, to support my boy. Imagine my surprise when Hudson was on live. And how do you think I felt when he had the opening skit? You know, the one where they say "Live from New York!" Not only that, but he had speaking parts as well—fourty-five full seconds of dialogue! See for yourself: http://www.nbc.com/saturday-night-live/video/mitt-romney-primaries-cold-open/138462. What the—?

Then he gets home all high and mighty and prances around the living room as Mom tells Dad that Hudson is only the second dog to have ever spoken live on SNL. Plus, he's the only Golden Retriever to hold this honor. Well, whoop-de-doo. Color me impressed. Oh, I sound a bit envious? Of course I am! Didn't you just read about the bang up job I did only weeks earlier that got cut? Wouldn't you be miffed? The worse part is that I can't help but feel proud of him at the same time... what a conundrum.

34

Say Aaahhh!

Germs! Yuck! I just discovered germs and am none too pleased. I know what you're thinking; as an RN, I should've been aware of them. However, I had no idea until Dad came home from Denver the other day where he went for work. As he walked through the door I could tell he looked somewhat worse for wear. He also sounded different, nasally somehow, though with that short nose I'm not sure how one can sound nasally. I mean, me, I've got a lot of nose with which to be nasally, but you people... I'm just saying.

Dad also kept making this awful coughing sound. I was perplexed and concerned by this strange behavior yet greeted him with my usual enthusiasm which includes a big wet one right on the old kisser just as he's trying to turn away. Anyhow, I then hear Mom asking Dad how he feels. Feels? I immediately go on to learn that there's such a thing as being sick. Well, not so immediate as I actually had to commandeer Mom's iPad, sneak it into my crate, and then proceed to read Google link after Google link about all things "sick". Germs, bacteria, ugh! They seem to cause all sorts of maladies such as clonorchiasis, aspergillosis, babesiosis, and don't even get me started on filariasis! It's enough to turn your stomach I tell you! The most troubling part is that many of these are zoonotic, a mind boggling sixty-one percent. I will definitely have to rethink my greeting ritual.

In order to further my education, I've taken to watching a weekly documentary on Netflix called "House". I'd heard of it before but thought it was about architects. Well, guess what? It's about a doctor, a European chap such as myself. This doctor's name is House, like I said, he's British but speaks like an American, go figure. Wouldn't he sound more sophisticated if he spoke like the Queen? Anyway, the more I watched the more concerned I got, not only for Dad but for myself. I've only been watching this documentary for a short time, however, from what I understand, germs and bacteria can be contagious. I expect to get sick at any moment. No, I'm not a hypochondriac. I kissed Dad, remember? This has turned me into a virtual petri dish.

I've cleared out my schedule for next week so I can nurse myself back to health should the need arise. I do have a trip planned to Target on Monday to buy Purell, Kleenex, Tylenol and a thermometer, to make myself a "woo is me" kit, if you will. It's possible that the initial osculum has not resulted in infection. Thus I've taken as many precautions as possible, you know, extra vitamin C

and frequent paw washing, to keep those minuscule para-
sites at bay. I haven't decided at which bay yet, perhaps
Tampa Bay...shout out to cousin Debbie. I've decided to
allow Mom to nurse Dad back to health, no need taking
any unnecessary risks. I'll be sleeping in the living room
for the foreseeable future. I shall return to the family bed-
chamber once he stops hacking and I'm not sick. Hmm,
you know what? Even if he stops hacking yet I am sick,
I shall return as well... after all, he's already had the bug
and Mom's apparently a risk taker. Come to think of it,
she didn't plant a wet one on his kisser when he got home
this time, so perhaps she's not as much of a risk taker as
I was led to believe.

35

February 26

I can't believe how excited I was to see myself on the big screen. Mom said that I needn't get that excited because television is not "the big screen". However, when I see myself on a fifty-five inch screen what am I supposed to call it? The little screen? So, what would you call an eight inch screen? Food for thought.

Anyway, there I was on TV in the Verizon commercial that is presently airing and that I've already shared with all of you. What I haven't shared are the details of the making of the commercial. I wasn't allowed to because of something Dad called a "confidentiality agreement". I don't know what he was talking about because I hadn't agreed to anything with anyone. In any event, I respected Dad's wishes. Now that it's airing I am free to give all the gory details.

Dad got me up at 7:00 in the morning and informed me that I needed to get ready for work. I was not pleased with having to get up early as I am not a morning dog. Plus, I would've appreciated the courtesy of a heads-up at least twenty-four hours in advance, thus I was not about to be rushed. After my morning decaf, nonfat, hazelnut latte, I decided that I'd comply with the plans made for me. I combed my hair, brushed my teeth and grabbed a new collateral. I wanted to look my spiffiest for what would become a nationally televised commercial.

We arrived on set promptly at 8:30 in the morning. There were so many people there. Cameras appeared out of thin air and "he's beautiful, what is he, can I take a picture, how much muppet is in him" was heard from every angle. This must be what Lassie felt. Puparazzi everywhere. Okay, they were just regular folks with cell phone cameras but you get the picture, no pun intended. Many of them wanted to be in the photo with me. I agreed and put on my sincerest smile though after a while it was more of an empty smirk. Then the work day began. First thing I was asked to do was jump up on an over three foot tall, stainless steel table. I had to jump from a stand, no running start because there was no room. I had to do it myself because, as I previously mentioned, they had not hired a stunt double. As I effortlessly made the leap, I could feel the looks of admiration from those around me. Everyone was impressed by both my athleticism and my willingness to please. Mom asked me to speak while on the table, so I did. The table immediately started wobbling violently. I soon discovered that it was on wheels. I was not at all pleased that it was moving so vowed not to speak on that table ever again. That would teach them to put me in an uncomfortable situation!

They locked the table legs and asked me to jump up on it a zillion more times. I complied every time. Even when Mom was at a considerable distance and I had to move away from her to do it. Yes, that's the type of guy I am. Then they had me run around the table a hundred and two times, followed by ripping paper, pulling a plant, and barking left and right. They even had me bark at an actress without any new cues from Mom or Dad. Dad was very supportive, he gave me constant bathroom breaks, while Mom kept fresh water in my bowl and had treats readily available. A few more times during my five hour— yes, *five!*—work day, they asked me to speak on the table. I refused. I'd already made it clear in no uncertain terms that this was not to be. A chap has to have principles.

While I enjoyed seeing the finished product, I was not pleased with the fact that I worked so long only to see a mere fourteen seconds of my footage used. Mom was upset too, yet Dad kept reminding us both that "it's a Verizon commercial, not a Chester commercial". As painful as it was to hear, I suppose he's right. Therefore, in the future, I shall require that my image appear in at least fifty percent of total content of any media jobs for which I am hired. That's more than reasonable, isn't it? I've drafted a list, a la Jennifer Lopez, of other non-negotiable conditions I will request. I shall require a private dressing room, no more "quiet corner, where he'll be out of the way" for this

Picard. I don't want to be harassed during my frequent mini yoga sessions. I also listed bottled water, PB&Js on whole wheat, freshly popped popcorn, and a fellow yogi with whom to practice as my on-set must haves. I shan't work again unless all these conditions are met.

36

March 04

"I solemnly swear that I am up to no good." I'm not sure why Dad says this every time Hudson and I are on the prowl. It's almost like a chant. He laughs as he says it, which seems odd to me. Why would being up to no good be amusing? He should be more annoyed than amused, but no, not Dad. I think Dad's off his rocker because he often calls me Harry Potter. There are two possible explanations for this: he's either, in fact, losing his mind or I remind him of Harry. I'm not sure who Harry is but, based on his last name, I'm assuming he's probably Dad's cousin. So maybe Dad is still sane and cousin Harry is a short hairy fellow. Ohhh... I get it, he's hairy. Okay, it's funny Dad.

From the way he speaks about him, it sounds like cousin Harry is not very well behaved, so I'm sure Dad says it in jest. Like when you say the opposite of what you mean. Mom, on the other hand, likens Hudson and me to "Zipi and Zape". I googled them because I don't know their last names so I'm not sure if they're related to us. I discovered that these two are iconic Spanish comic book characters created in 1947. I heard Mom telling Dad that she used to watch the cartoon in the 80s when she lived in Spain. Zipi and Zape are fraternal twins, they are short and have evil grins. One is blond and one is brunette, thus Mom refers to Hudson as Zipi and to me as Zape. These two siblings are domestic terrors who cause chaos and all sorts of pandemonium. That said, I have no idea why Mom would call us that. What would prompt her to make that association? I see a trend in Mom and Dad's comparisons, a trend that makes me somewhat uncomfortable. They normally make these comparisons when we work in cahoots (their word, not mine).

Case in point, if Mom and Dad are fortunate enough to have time for an afternoon nap, Hudson will inevitably need something, anything really. Is it his fault that he needs water, bathroom break, play, food, hug during that half hour? And is it my fault that once Hudson gets "asked" to "go lie down, now" I need something immediately thereafter? I think not. This just happens folks. Haven't you heard of a coincidence? By the same token, so what if Hudson sees something outside and starts barking when Mom is on the phone? Then Hudson stops barking and I continue, lest Mom should not realize that there's a person, dog, or butterfly outside. So what? Yes, maybe we've unwittingly mastered the tag team art, but it's a coincidence I tell you.

I happened to come across an e-mail from Amazon

the other day. It was an order confirmation for the "Zipi y Zape" comic books, in Spanish. Apparently, Mom expects Hudson and me to read them, probably in the hopes that we'll start behaving. I'm sure she means behaving differently because we already behave well. Anyway, she wants Hudson and me to read? Read? What's wrong with this picture? How can Hudson and I read? The books are in Spanish! Sometimes Mom doesn't put her thinking cap on in the morning. Seriously Mom, you can't just go ordering willy-nilly online. I guess she'll have to read them to us at night when she tucks us in. I don't know about you, but I certainly enjoy a warm glass of milk and a bedtime story. I don't think I'll enjoy my bedtime story as much as I should tonight as I'm a bit upset. You see, my cohort was live on SNL again last night. (Perhaps I am encouraging Mom and Dad's comparisons by calling Hudson my cohort... mental note to measure my adjectives.) Anyway, as per usual, Hudson's appearance on Saturday Night Live, pre-taped or live, has left me feeling disgruntled. As you may recall, Hudson did the "cold open" on SNL a mere three weeks ago. After that appearance, Hudson and I had a long talk and I thought we had agreed that we'd take turns on SNL, so this was my turn. That was obviously not his understanding. Time for another talk. However, in the spirit of brotherhood, I am once again compelled to share his success.

Counter Attack

37

I am so proud of myself because I learn very quickly. Well, not only for that, it's just one of many reasons. Let me list them for you, first—no, I'd better not, this is a diary not an encyclopedia.

As I'm sure you recall, in January during the filming of the Verizon commercial, I was taught that it was okay to jump up on a table. This week, I put that knowledge to good use on our kitchen counter. Mom ordered some angry bird toys for Hudson and me and gave us one each. She left the other ones on the counter out of our reach, presumably to give to us at a later time. Later time? What was she thinking? Seize the moment, Mom! These birds are the bomb. They make noise when we squeeze them and they're shaped like balls so we can play retrieve with them in the house. Plus, they're soft enough that Dad doesn't have to fear being struck in the head by a rogue one when Mom throws them for us down the hall in her usual MLB worthy style.

I played with mine for a while, however soon decided that I wanted to inspect the other ones, lest they should be better. I put my two front paws on the counter but, alas, could not reach the toys. Not to be deterred, I remembered that I was able to take superman like vertical leaps from a standing position. The counter is thirty-seven inches high. I calculated for wind and up I went, easy peasy. Wow, the house looked so different from up there. Look at that, a sink, dog treats, toaster, blender, coffee pot; cool! I stayed there for quite a while, surveying my domain. I walked around a bit though not enough to fully investigate all of it. I knew Mom and Dad wouldn't mind because they were very proud of me when I did it for the commercial.

Down the hall comes Mom and sees me on the counter. Our eyes meet as she looks up at me and I look down at her. I flash my choppers at her and she immediately starts giggling, then gets her phone to take a picture. She takes the picture and asks me to get off the counter. If it's so amusing and I too am enjoying myself, why do I have to get off? "There's still so much to inspect," I say, but being the compliant chap that I am, off I go. Then Dad comes home that evening and Mom tells him all about it.

He's like "What's the big deal? He gets on the counter all the time." Mom's like "No, I mean *on* the counter, with all fours." He's like "No way." Mom's like "Yeah." Dad's like "Unbelievable!" Mom's like "Check it out. Chester, table."

Table is my command to jump onto something,

whatever Mom's pointing at. So up I jump, once again effortlessly and gracefully, even if I do say so myself. Dad was so impressed. Then they asked me to get off the counter and that's when disaster stuck. I slipped and, though I didn't hurt myself, I got a bit scared. Yes, I am comfortable enough with my masculinity to admit that I was scared.

"Uh-oh" said Dad. "Yikes" said Mom. "We'd better get him back up there or we won't be able to get him to jump onto objects when we need him to." The poor things proceed to spend the next twenty minutes begging me to get back up. Didn't they remember how put out I was by the Verizon table on wheels? I don't want to jump onto or off of anything that I perceive as moving or as not affording me the necessary traction for my cat-like abilities.

After much coaxing, many treats and a carefully placed mat, I finally relented and jumped back on it. I have now overcome my fear and jump on the counter every time they ask me. Little do they know that this was a carefully crafted plan to ensure that I don't get in trouble any time they catch me in flagrante on the counter. Dance, puppets, dance. I believe I shall use this manipulative behavior for all my desires in the future. I will be able to get away with anything. (Insert evil laugh here.) As a matter of fact, I put my theory to the test already as I encored this behavior with the agility tunnel. I've been pretending to be afraid of it ever since they introduced it to me a few months ago, yet today I allowed Dad to "convince" me to take it for the first time. You see, I will now be able to take wrong course tunnels in agility any time my little heart desires and will not be chastised for it.

Show Time

38

I went to my first conformation dog show last weekend, unfortunately, it was not as I'd expected. We drove to Pennsylvania on Friday night and checked into a hotel. It had been months since I'd been in a hotel, so I felt the need to bark at every sound I heard, and I mean every sound. Dad kept asking me to be quiet. Doesn't he want me to alert them to suspicious sounds? Well, these were all suspicious to me. I finally settled down and we got a good night's sleep.

We got up bright and early on Saturday and off to the show we went. The excitement was palpable. Dad had a bunch of camera equipment with him, undoubtedly to take pictures of my debut. Upon arrival to the show site, I noticed that most of the dogs were smaller than I. I've heard that they don't measure at breed shows, too bad because none of these dogs fit our breed standard regarding size. I wasn't too concerned because I was sure the judge would notice without the need to measure and I'd take WD, BOW and BISS by default. Since we were early, Mom put me in a crate as Dad set up his camera equipment. He had a lot of stuff, even a backdrop and flashes on stands. It seemed a bit excessive but it was my first breed show so it wasn't a total surprise. Suddenly, I hear what I think is the show starting and off goes Dad, camera in hand telling us that sweeps are in the ring. Mom stays behind only long enough to take her coat off. Then she walks away leaving Morgan and me in the crate together. Maybe I'd have to wait until they finished sweeping the ring.

They come back after a while and Dad starts fidgeting with his computer and camera equipment. It appeared that he'd taken some pictures, most likely to gauge the lighting to ensure that I was well lit when my turn came. Then the regular classes begin and again they both walk away without me. This was getting annoying. Mom comes back a few times to check on us but never actually takes me to the ring. After what seems like days, though might have only been a few hours, I see a bunch of people coming into my room carrying their dogs and holding rosettes. Dad pulls out a sign, puts it on the podium and I read "Delaware Valley Chinese Crested Club"—what? Of course, all these dogs looked familiar because they were Cresteds like Morgan, not because they were Picards. This show is just for Cresteds? So what am I doing here?

Dad proceeds to take two zillion pictures of dogs he calls "winners" as Morgan and I are forced to watch from our crate. Well, I'll have none of this. No sooner does he finish photographing the "winners" (where's Charlie

Sheen?), that I voice my displeasure about not being pho-
tographed on the podium. As Mom allows me out of the
crate, I run over and jump onto the raised platform and
I get my wish, a winner's shot. What did I win, you ask?
Hello! I won the right to have my picture taken on the
podium! After my photo is taken, Mom stacks me a few
times and has people go over me, disrespectful people at
that. They look in my mouth, perhaps for spinach I might
have missed while flossing. They touch me all over, ALL
over, even my privates. Nothing hidden down there, folks.
Mom and I will have a serious discussion about this later.
I don't enjoy being stacked and I show my displeasure
repeatedly... put my foot where? Stay? What does that
mean? Look in that direction? I will look where ever I
please, thank you very much.

That night back at the hotel, I am not as chatty as
usual. This was not at all what I expected. I thought my
chance had come to strut my stuff in the ring, not just
stand there like cattle to be branded. I am more than disappointed. I spend all Saturday night plotting my revenge.
I know! I'll wake them earlier than my normal time of
7:30. Ha! That'll teach them. I wake up once at 6:20 and
figure I can still get another 10 minutes sleep. I'm just
dozing off when the alarm goes off. What??? Immediately
Mom and Dad get out of bed and start complaining about
the time change. They mention something about daylight
savings time. What are we saving time for? In any event,

I decide I shall adjust my inner clock and wake them up extra early on Monday. And come Monday morning I do just that. You see, my normal morning routine consists of waking as soon as I hear my upstairs neighbor's footsteps. He gets up at 7:00 am and starts the day with some heavy walking around his apartment. Once awake, I greet the day with a few minutes of light stretching, scratching and licking. If I happen to be in a deep sleep cycle when the footsteps commence, either Morgan or my Golden sister Kelly see to it that I wake up. I then jump on the bed, landing willy nilly where I may, but always on a limb or other body part. I shall make a point of stepping on Dad's privates from now on. Let's see how *he* likes it!

I walk all around the bed to ensure my folks wake up. I show no concern as to where I put my feet, show no weakness, I say. If there's any doubt as to if I'm accomplishing my wake-up mission, I go over to Morgan, who sleeps on the bed, and use her as a makeshift alarm clock. As I approach, she immediately starts emitting this low rumbling sound. In order to make certain that no one is still snoozing, I have only to move in closer for a little sniff, it never fails, Morgan immediately lets out a blood curdling scream that would make a vociferous baboon proud. This unfailingly wakes Mom and Dad. Ah, time for breakfast and a run on the waterfront.

March 18

Happy third birthday to my Golden brother, best friend, and mentor Hudson. I got so excited when I heard it was going to be his birthday yesterday that I decided to throw him a surprise party. I planned it all out by myself. I bought balloons, a birthday hat, a number "3" candle; I even baked him a cake. What I didn't do was buy a birthday gift or send out party invitations... I guess planning it all by myself wasn't such a good idea, was it? I didn't know that it's tradition to give gifts at birthday parties nor had I any idea that one has to invite people. It's his third birthday for goodness sake. Didn't anyone remember from last year? Why would I have to send out reminders? In any event, due to my faux paw, Hudson and I were the only party guests. I did make a point to tell Kelly and Morgan about it but they said they were unable to attend. They mentioned something about being on a diet. Mom and Dad made a brief appearance to sing "happy birthday" and take a picture, but that's it. Guess they were too busy to sit for a piece of cake and celebrate this once-a-year event of which we have so few.

I'd be remiss if I didn't admit that Mom did help me earlier in the week to bake and frost the cake. I'm still honing my cooking skills and haven't quite mastered the oven controls so I welcomed her help. Dad chipped in too, he helped inflate the balloons. He made it look so easy that I thought I'd give it a try. Good grief, you can't imagine how difficult it was. First of all, I couldn't wrap my lips around them. Which begs the question, do chickens have balloons at their birthday parties? Anyway, when I finally got my lips around one, I sucked it in and almost choked. As I stood there gagging, Dad laughed and told me that I was suppose to blow into it. That information would've been useful forty seconds ago Dad! So, I picked up another balloon and blew. I must have blown too violently because suddenly the balloon goes flying out of my mouth and hits Morgan square on the kisser. I laughed and laughed until the balloons were confiscated. Where was Dad's sense of humor now?

All laughed out after my choking incident, are we? I tell you, these people have no sense of humor when it really counts. None the less, Hudson and I had fun at the party. We ate cake and then played chase the balloon. I was able to catch and pop three of them myself. They are surprisingly thin skinned. Hudson was touched by my thoughtfulness and even promised to plan a surprise party for me next month. Surprise? Well, it's the thought that counts. He's more worldly than I, so I'm sure he knows all about the invitations. Perhaps I'll buy some and leave them on his bed just in case. I'd really like to have a big turnout because it'll be my first birthday and I want to make it count. I'd also enjoy receiving lots of gifts and I've done the math: the more people, the more gifts. In light of that, I shall ask Hudson to invite everyone we know.

April 01

As I'm sure you recall, I worked with children on my second job with The Company Kids catalog a couple of months ago. The shoot was for the Spring 2012 issue that I've not yet seen as Mom, in her efficient as usual manner, has been unable to obtain a copy. My two-footed co-stars in that shoot were displeased at having to work with yours truly. No doubt because they were concerned that my mere presence was a sure fire way for them to go all but unnoticed.

Ever since that shoot, I have been paying close attention to children. I've noticed an alarming trend in the behavior of the great majority of kids, present company excluded. There are many adjectives that I could use to describe most rug rats... well-behaved would not be one of them. No, they seem to be more entitled than generous, more defiant than obedient, and definitely much ruder than polite. I don't get it. My four footed counterparts and I are expected to behave in any situation, even those in which our instinct should get the better of us. Why the double standard? All I'm saying is that if my fellow canines and I behaved in this manner we'd be thrown a proverbial beating. The scariest part of this situation is that it seems to be international. I would know, I've been to Pennsylvania, Connecticut and New York. Don't get me wrong, I love munchkins, and not just the type you buy at Dunkin' Donuts. I sidle up to them any chance I get. I enjoy the kindness I see in some kids' eyes and the sweet caress some moppets bestow upon me. There's really nothing like the honest affection of a child, I highly recommend being in the presence of those types of bambinos. Unfortunately, those are the minority of the cases. More often than not, you get pushed around, yelled at and even have the occasional foot flung in your general direction. When did parents stop paying attention? When did manners become so out of style? When did the word "no" become a four letter word? (I'm not the greatest mathematician, however by my count, it's still two letters, isn't it?) Why is disciplining tykes taboo but disciplining a dog expected? When did I become so philosophical? If you don't believe me when I describe the sorry state of today's youth and you don't want to sit in a courtroom, just go to a school yard at recess. Watch them interact for a while, then go to a dog show where you'll see hundreds of canines behaving in close proximity to one another for hours and compare behaviors. Yes, sometimes we too get grouchy, hot, tired, annoyed even. The difference is that when we do, most of us don't automatically resort to personal injury. We give each other a look, a growl, perhaps show our teeth, sans spinach natch. That's usually as far as it goes. On the other hand, ankle-biters (and I'm not referring to Chihuahuas) choose violence far too often. I've noticed that the most considerate whipper snappers I've met share their lives with a dog. Coincidence? I think not. It might be a good idea to encourage all parents to bestow upon their little ones the behavioral advantage of being raised with a hairy sibling, or in Morgan's case, a hairless sibling. We teach by example and really folks, is there any better way?

April 08

Mom spent all week prepping for a trip to Spain to visit my grandma Luz. Come Thursday, she packed her bag and gave Morgan a bath. I was so excited that I would be going to Spain and become acquainted with my European roots. I, too, had planned ahead and had gone to Target to buy Dramamine. I've heard of air sickness and didn't want to fall victim to this horrendous affliction. Though I am somewhat confused about it because I've never gotten sick from breathing air, why take the chance and risk having it ruin my vacay?

I packed my passport, a change of collateral, comb, toothbrush and the Dramamine. I know about the travel restrictions on toothpaste so I decided I'd just buy some there. Even though I noticed that Dad, Kelly and Hudson weren't packing, I didn't think much of it until Thursday afternoon. I wondered if Mom and Dad had forgotten about me, as they left the house with Morgan, destination airport, and closed the door behind them before I even had a chance to grab my bag. I watched through the window as they got in the car and drove off. Then it hit me, I was expected to stay behind.

Once the shock wore off, I unpacked. As I was taking the Dramamine to the bathroom, I started feeling sadder and sadder. I'm an ideal travel companion. I'm up on all current events and make nice conversation. I have lovely breath and know when to sit quietly. Why didn't they want my company? As a tear rolled down my face, I realized that that's what the Dramamine was for: drama. How could I have not noticed earlier? After all, it's in the name "Drama Mine". So I opened the package and took one. Though it didn't help me feel happier, I did have a lovely nap.

I was just starting to dream about Picans when in the door come Mom, Dad and Morgan. Apparently, Dad was the chauffeur for Mom and Morgan who were the ones scheduled to travel, yet here they were, all three of them. As I understand it, they were going stand-by because Dad works for an airline. Mom was disappointed that they'd been unable to board the plane due to the fact that it was overbooked. What part of stand-by doesn't Mom get? There's a reason it's not called "fly-by". Mom and Morgan stood by as the airplane left without them. How was that outcome unexpected?

Anywho, speaking of Picans. I've seen a bunch of weird looking dogs lately. You know, mixed breeds. The press calls them "designer dogs". What are they designed to do? Deceive people into spending money on a dog with unpredictable characteristics, shady health clearances and papers of an unknown registry. The worst part is that un-educated consumers pay lots of money to purchase them. The more ridiculous the name, the more expensive the designer breed.

I was thinking about this when the Dramamine kicked in and I fell asleep. I dreamt about a lovely young lady I'd met, Rihanna. She is from Afghanistan. Just think about the beautiful designer babies we could make together and what people would be willing to pay. All I needed to do was to come up with a silly name. Hmm, what would you get when you mixed a Picard with an Afghan? Why a Pic-an, of course! Brilliant! I told Dad, who seemed unim-pressed as he mumbled something about it being an ap-propriate name for my offspring. Mom was more blunt. "Your puppies would be nuts," she said, "just like their father." I wonder what they were implying...

Airborne

42

Time really does fly. If you don't believe me, just ask Dad. He always takes his watch with him when he flies. I wonder if Dad taught it to fly too. Does it have a pilots' license like Dad does?

I tried getting time to fly once myself. I launched a watch as far as I could off our deck and, believe you me, it did achieve flight for a good twenty feet, almost as far as my flight path over the agility broad jump while training.

This year has flown by too. And what a year it's been! I've just had my first birthday, sans party by the way—thanks Hudson! Now it's time to reflect on my life. I was born in New Jersey to parents of French descent. Mom and Dad put me up for adoption, I don't know why, perhaps we were too many mouths to feed. Perhaps Dad was a merchant marine and Mom a traveling nurse and, really, that's no life for a child. In any event, my adoptive parents are wonderful people. They give me love, food, a warm bed and are just busy enough to afford me the freedom I crave for self discovery. Ah, yes, I've been on many an adventure. Just me, my PB&J, sunglasses (invaluable when trying to disguise oneself) and the open road. Through these adventures, I discovered feature films, ferry travel and shopping in Manhattan... or not, whatever the case may be. I became a member of Gamblers' Anonymous; as it turns out casino ownership was not for me. I learned that destroying other people's property, such as shoes, is only fun for the destroyer and not for the property owner. This type of destruction can send one on a guilt trip; even the second, third and fourth time that one attempts it. Who would've thought? Maybe that's the reason I was shot at the vet's office in December, it could've been revenge.

I learned valuable lessons. For example, did you know that popcorn "pieces" have different ranks? I also learned while helping paint our living room walls, that selfless acts can be very rewarding. I learned that education is an important part of a well rounded individual, thus I've amassed a library that would make even Shakespeare jealous. At five months old I got my CGC, followed by my RN only two months later. I believe this made me the youngest Picard in the history of the AKC to achieve this honor, and I beat Hudson's record by a month. Take that Mr. "Oops I forgot all about your birthday!" Plus, I'm most likely the youngest Picard with a driver's license, at least in New Jersey.

I successfully dodged the flu virus and never got a DUI. I cheered Morgan on to her MACH and held her ribbons for her official photo. I even showed my support when Hudson took some of my acting gigs. I enjoyed my first Thanksgiving, sans the bird mind you, and Christmas avec the gifts thank goodness. I learned the hard way that a tree in the house is by no means carte blanche for using the bathroom indoors.

I shared a gingerbread latte with Mom and grandma at a lovely outdoor cafe. Unfortunately, I had to learn about the despair of loss, through the death of my sister Desi, followed by the disappointment of rejection, as I dabbled in different career paths. I started out as a thespian, I applied most unsuccessfully to culinary school, but I was very successful in my brief stint as a private eye.

Only last year, I was a small, floppy-eared, goofy kid whose teeth were stolen. In this short time, I've become the humble, breathtakingly handsome, large-eared, worldly, first-class party-planning gentleman you see before you. Or after you, depending on where you're standing in relation to me. I've yet to get a stamp on my passport though, which I vow to do this year.

Full circle back to my thespian roots, I've already starred in print ads and the small screen, though not in the recurring sitcom role that I so desire. I've done so much in this short time and have so many dreams yet to be realized, not the least of which is to conquer the silver screen. In light of this, I have revised my on-set "must-haves" list. I think it was too demanding and may have thwarted many a job opportunity. I look forward to the coming year and the adventures that lay before me. I vow to cherish every moment life gives me, every family member, every friend, every smile. I will welcome with open arms all the training and competitive events that Mom and Dad have planned for me, within reason, of course. Let's not get carried away. I'm a Picard and, as such, I have a mind of my own and the intelligence to know how to use it.

April 22

Another adventure, though this time an adventure gone terribly wrong. Last night, as I watched Mom and Dad prepare to go out, I wondered if they were planning on taking me with them. They were talking about Radio City Music Hall and the show they were going to see, some comedian named Ron White. I would certainly enjoy seeing a comedian. I have a fantastic sense of humor and might even learn a thing or two from this guy.

I started to panic a bit when they put Hudson and me in their bedroom, said "let's leave him out of the crate this time" and shut the door behind them. My worst fears were realized as I watched them drive out of the garage, destination ferry. Were they leaving me behind again? I was having none of this! I sprung into action, opened the door, grabbed my bag and chased them down the street. Luckily, I always have a bag packed with essentials, like a fresh PBJ and sunglasses. Just as I suspected, they pulled into the ferry parking lot, so I knew they were going into the city. I donned my sunglasses and followed them at a safe distance, ensuring my incognito-ness by taking cover when needed. I used natural elements such as trees and lampposts, and they were none the wiser to my presence.

On a Saturday evening the ferry is jam packed with theater goers, so I was undetected. I lost sight of them a few times as it was difficult to see at night while wearing sunglasses, but wasn't concerned because the ferry doesn't make stops between Jersey and Manhattan. Think about it, why would anyone disembark in the middle of the Hudson? That's ludicrous unless you're a fish and, if you're a fish, why would you be on the ferry to begin with?

So I boarded the ferry and went to the top floor to allow the wind to blow through my hair at will. I love the feel of the ocean breeze through my whiskers. I was surprised when we got to the other side of the river and discovered I was unfamiliar with my surroundings. I chalked it up to the time that had lapsed since my last ferry adventure. I boarded one of the buses, destination Radio City. I couldn't see Mom and Dad on the bus as it pulled out and started wondering where they were sitting. I began to doubt my choice of bus, when I found myself dozing off. It'd been a long day.

I'd gotten up at 6:00 am to accompany the family to an agility trial. A trial at which I was disallowed participation. I keep telling them I'd love to try trialing, to no avail, they ignore my every plea. But I digress, I woke up what seemed like a few minutes later, only to find myself in utterly unfamiliar surroundings. The bus stopped and we all got off. I started walking around somewhat aimlessly. Wait a minute, this was starting to look familiar after all. I'd been here before. Was this…? No, it couldn't be—this was Coney Island. Mom brought me here months ago to film a commercial for Kewpie mayonnaise. How'd I end up here? I guess donning sunglasses at night had some visual disadvantages I'd not foreseen. How would I get back to Manhattan? Oh my, now I was sure to miss Ron White.

Dejected, I made my way back to Jersey. I don't think I took the shortest route as I crossed the Verrazano bridge, Staten Island and the Bayonne bridge back into New Jersey. Two hours later, I arrived at home. Kelly and Morgan ran to the front door as I came into the house. It was obvious by their disappointment that they expected to see Mom and Dad. Hudson, on the other hand, greeted me with a huge smile when I went into the bedroom. He was so happy to see me and I was so relieved to be home, that we immediately started playing. We jumped on and off the furniture, tore at the bedskirt, pulled clothes out of the hamper and basically ran amuck. We had just started to clean up the mess when Mom and Dad got home.

For some reason, they were displeased with the fun we'd had. Mom questioned our choices. "We left them a lot of toys, yet they chose not to play with them." Why, pray tell dear Mom, would we play with the toys we're allowed to play with then you're here? Why not try playing with something otherwise forbidden? "Well, I suppose he's not ready to be trusted out of the crate for extended periods of time," Dad said. Was he talking about me?

April 29

I did it! I've joined the age of social media and finally got myself a Facebook account: you can friend me at "Chester Gi Golo".

I'm excited because I've got many friends with whom I can now be in touch 168. One hundred and sixty eight what, you ask? I don't really know, but that's what you get when you multiply 24 times 7, really it is, I used a calculator to figure that out. You see, I've not been able to update my friends as much as I'd like because I haven't mastered the use of telephones of any kind. Placing a phone call or sending a text message has always been a challenge for me, I chalk it up to my huge paws. Typing on a laptop is easier due to the size of the keys and now, what with spellcheck, words practically type themselves. Sometimes the incorrect words type themselves and then you sound like you've imbibed.

In any event, FB seems to be a good medium for me to keep in touch with my peeps. In case you're wondering, I wanted to go with my stage name. I applied for Chester Gigolo but it would seem that the FB people are a smidgeon of a pigeon uptight when it comes to certain words. They wouldn't allow "Gigolo". Why? Do they think that it's a bad word? Listen, I'm not one to have a foul mouth. Unless by foul mouth you mean chicken breath, in which case then, yes I do have a foul mouth. And why, pray tell, is that a bad thing? I could call you spaghetti breath just as easily. In any event, the FB powers that be nixed "Gigolo" so I had to outsmart them by putting a space in it. I was annoyed at first but, now that I've had time to digest it, I think it gives me a certain *je ne sais quoi*.

I've learned a lot in my short time as a Facebookie. I've learned the art of graffiti, you know, writing on walls. I've also learned how to post photos and suspect I will put this skill to use often. I had trouble at first while trying to upload my profile photo. I had to battle the internet imps, they won and uploaded it a bunch of times just to spite me, though I suppose that's not a such a bad thing with a mug like mine. I'll add photos when I get a chance. I shall also express my thoughts, dreams and opinions at will. Mom says that people might disagree with my opinions. She tells me not to take offense if that happens. The way I see it, they're my opinions and as such are beyond contestation. Dad said that I'm only allowed to stay on FB as long as I understand that he will periodically monitor my usage. I've decided to acquiesce to his request because it seems easier than starting an argument that would no doubt develop into a battle of the wills and, really, who has the time or energy for that? I've been spreading myself too thin as it is, much like the peanut butter on my PBJs when I'm in a hurry.

In light of this, I have some disconcerting news that may come as a shock to some of you. As of today, I will temporarily discontinue my weekly diary. I've decided to take my writing skills to the next level and shall commence writing an autobiography at once. It will be an in-depth tell all which I suspect will ruffle a few feathers once it's published. I want to thank all of you for your support and comments. I hope that you will continue to support me as I embark in this new chapter, pun intended, of my life.

Epilogue

Thank you for reading my book and sharing in my adventures. As you have probably guessed, some of the aforementioned adventures may have been slightly influenced by my vivid imagination. You might even say that a few are outright figments. The parts about being an athlete, actor, and author are true, though perhaps somewhat exaggerated. However, I can attest to the fact that truth is often stranger than fiction and usually more humiliating. My real life is chock full of excitement and I rarely have a chance to just sit back and relax. I find that daydreaming is a great release for the stress of my busy life. One of my most ambitious dreams is to write an autobiography—a dream I intend to make a reality as early as this fall… stay tuned.

About The Author

Christina was born an Army brat in Stuttgart, Germany. Her father was from Alabama and her mother is from Madrid, Spain. Though her parents were animal lovers, the frequent moves of a military family made dog ownership an impossibility.

The first time she shared her life with a dog was when she met her Thai-born husband Taylor, son of US missionaries, and his two-and-a-half-year-old Golden Retriever Bogart. Bogart was her constant companion and quickly earned a permanent spot in her heart. He was a true gentleman of dogs and was infinitely patient with her mistakes. That was four dog generations, twenty-five years and four breeds ago. Each dog taught her something different: from therapy work, through competitive canine companion sports, to advertising and film work.

Her first step out of "pet only" ownership was an obedience class she took just for fun with Bogart's son Cooper. Little did she know that it would set her on the path to many new and interesting adventures in the world of canines. She and her husband competed in obedience and agility with Kelly and Cooper's son Gable. They also dabbled in therapy work and, as a matter of fact, it was at a seminar for therapy dog certification twelve years ago that one of the speakers told them about her dog's acting career. This piqued Christina's interest and a few days later she met with an animal agent in New York city. Gable started working the following week and she now has the title of "animal wrangler" firmly ensconced in her resume with print ads, three feature films and countless commercials. All her dogs have been bitten by the acting bug, so it's no surprise that Gable's son Hudson is following in his father's footsteps.

Ten years ago, Christina strayed from the Golden Retriever world when she got her Afghan Hound Desi. Desi introduced her to rally, lure coursing and conformation shows, and, while she didn't excel in any of these, it was thanks to her that Chinese Crested Morgan joined the family. Morgan recently became one of only six Cresteds in the United States to have gotten both a breed championship and an agility championship. One day, while on the American Kennel Club website, Christina discovered the Berger Picard. After extensive research of this intriguing breed, she knew that the puppy soon-to-be known as Chester would further enrich her life.

All the classes and professional training she obtained, including a Master's Degree in Canine Psychology, have not taught her as much as her eight dogs have. She is thankful for the patience, understanding and unconditional love they have given her and strives to make herself worthy of them every day. It is truly rewarding for her to see the look of satisfaction in her dogs' eyes when they learn to negotiate obstacles in agility or learn new tricks for media work. Though she and her husband Taylor are busy with their "regular" jobs (he as a commercial pilot, she as a federal court interpreter) they make time to train daily. Every moment not spent at work is dedicated to the four dogs who currently share their lives.

CPSIA information can be obtained at www.ICGtesting.com
Printed in the USA
LVOW041542090812

293688LV00011B/6/P